RESOURC
BOOKS FC
TEACHERS

series editor
ALAN MALEY

LETTERS

Nicky Burbidge, Peta Gray,
Sheila Levy, and Mario Rinvolucri

Oxford University Press

Oxford University Press, Great Clarendon Street, Oxford OX2 6DP

Oxford New York
Athens Auckland Bangkok Bogota Bombay Buenos Aires
Calcutta Cape Town Dar es Salaam Delhi Florence Hong Kong
Istanbul Karachi Kuala Lumpur Madras Madrid Melbourne
Mexico City Nairobi Paris Singapore Taipei Tokyo Toronto Warsaw
and associated companies in
Berlin Ibadan

Oxford and *Oxford English* are trade marks of
Oxford University Press

ISBN 0 19 442149 X

© Oxford University Press

First published 1996
Second impression 1997

Set by Wyvern Typesetting Ltd., Bristol

Printed in Hong Kong

Photocopying

Acknowledgements

We would like to thank a wide network of colleagues for many of the ideas that have fed this book, especially people at the Cambridge Academy of English and Pilgrims English Language Courses. We also want to thank students and teacher trainees at both schools for helping us to develop our ideas; they often produced eye-opening texts in response to the frames that we offered.

We would like to thank examinations boards for the letter-writing climate that they have created by using this format so widely in their testing procedures.

Finally, we would like to thank Internet technology for making this book up-to-date.

The publisher and authors would like to thank the following for their kind permission to use extracts from copyright material. There are instances where we have been unable to trace or contact the copyright holder before our printing deadline. We apologize for this apparent negligence. If notified the publisher will be pleased to rectify any errors or omissions at the earliest opportunity.

The Economist: mailing letter dated August 1991

Faber and Faber Ltd and Random House, Inc. for an extract from 'Night Mail' by W. H. Auden from *Collected Poems* edited by Edward Mendelsohn, copyright © 1976 by Edward Mendelsohn, William Meredith, and Monroe K. Spears, Executors of the Estate of W. H. Auden.

Innovations Group plc for a Christmas mailing letter

Michelin Tyre Company for a letter

W. W. Norton & Company, Inc. for a letter from *Dear Bess: The Letters from Harry to Bess Truman 1910–1959* edited by Robert H. Ferrell, copyright © 1983 by Robert H. Ferrell

Penguin Books Ltd. and the Peters, Fraser, and Dunlop Group Ltd. for the letter dated Saturday 11th March 1967 from *A Particular Friendship* by Dirk Bogarde (Viking 1989), copyright © Labofilms SA 1989

The Rockingham Press for 'Letter for Yannis Ritsos' by Özdemir Ince translated by Feyyaz Kayacan Fergar from F. K. Fergar: *Modern Turkish Poetry* (1992).

The authors and publisher would like to thank Denise Bardan, Valerie Davis, Tim Herdon, Alan Love, Barbara Mason, Helen Milavsky, Carol Miller, and Claire Stringer for their kind permission to reproduce personal letters.

Contents

The authors and series editor

Nicky Burbidge has taught in Greece, Portugal, and Italy. She worked as teacher and examinations officer at the Cambridge Academy of English for several years, but is now based at Bilkent University in Ankara, Turkey, where she teaches pre-sessional English.

Peta Gray has a background in professional theatre and sociolinguistics. She has a particular interest in teaching schoolphobic teenagers. She also specializes in helping Japanese students adapt to life in the UK, the area covered in her forthcoming book written with Sue Leather.

Sheila Levy taught French and English to secondary school students and adults in the north of England before becoming an EFL teacher in 1986. She started up the Community Liaison Scheme at the Cambridge Academy of English, maximizing the contact of foreign students with the English-speaking world around them. She has been Director of Studies at the Cambridge Academy since 1994.

Mario Rinvolucri started work as a teacher of EFL in 1964. He has written many books for teachers, among them *Challenge to Think* (with Marge Berer and Christine Frank), *Vocabulary* (with John Morgan), and *Video* (with Richard Cooper and Mike Lavery). While *Letters* was being developed, he was teaching at the Cambridge Academy of English, but he is now back at Pilgrims English Language Courses in Canterbury, England.

Alan Maley worked for The British Council from 1962 to 1988, serving as English Language Officer in Yugoslavia, Ghana, Italy, France, and China, and as Regional Representative for the British Council in South India (Madras). From 1988 to 1993 he was Director General of the Bell Educational Trust, Cambridge. He is currently Senior Fellow in the Department of English Language and Literature of the National University of Singapore. He has written *Literature*, in this series (with Alan Duff), *Beyond Words*, *Sounds Interesting*, *Sounds Intriguing*, *Words*, *Variations on a Theme*, and *Drama Techniques in Language Learning* (all with Alan Duff), *The Mind's Eye* (with Françoise Grellet and Alan Duff), and *Learning to Listen* and *Poem into Poem* (with Sandra Moulding). He is also Series Editor for the Oxford Supplementary Skills series.

Foreword

EFL has been characterized for much of its lifespan by a healthy wish for innovation. This has often paid dividends, but it may occasionally have diverted our attention from more obvious sources of inspiration. Letters are a good example of this 'neglect through familiarity' phenomenon (the spectacles we cannot find because they are on the end of our nose).

They offer at least four major advantages to the EFL teacher: availability, variety, relevance, and interest:

— It is relatively easy, even in low-resource environments, to lay hands on a variety of letters.
— The major genre of 'letter' comprises a wonderful variety of sub-genres. In the words of W. H. Auden:

> Letters of thanks, letters from banks,
> Letters of joy from girl and boy,
> Receipted bills and invitations
> To inspect new stock or visit relations,
> And applications for situations
> And timid lovers' declarations
> And gossip, gossip from all the nations …

— Letters are also clearly relevant to students, both in terms of their personal pay-off and their future usefulness in real-life situations.

— Relevance, combined with students' natural human curiosity, gives them a definite advantage in motivational attraction.

This set of activities for capitalizing on the use of letters is far removed from the humdrum 'use this letter as a model to write' format. The activities give a creative twist to the use of the letter form, often by giving the students a personal stake in the outcome. Not least, students are led to the writing of 'real' letters, which opens the door to the enormously rich possibilities for email between individuals and classes on an international scale.

Alan Maley

Introduction

Why letters?

If you look through the teacher resource book genre that has grown from the seeds that Bill Lee, Alan Maley and Alan Duff, Donn Byrne, and Andrew Wright planted in the seventies, you will see that some books usefully import fresh ideas into language teaching from feeder fields such as drama, maths, and psychodrama. Other resource books choose to look at areas within language teaching itself—for example storytelling and dictation—and find fresh ways of exploiting them. Letter writing is one such area. It is clearly not as ancient a use of language as storytelling, but it dates back a long way.

We feel there is a crying need to humanize the writing class. How can there be writers without readers? It is very hard to write and speak to people you don't know and who aren't there. No one writes a letter to nobody (very few folk, anyway): the addressee is central in the writer's mind. Writing letters is also a way into the fascinating world of inner monologue which is the breeding ground of writing. Some personal letters seem really to be stretches of inner monologue shared with the addressee.

We also feel that there is a need to humanize the reading class. Often a reading text isn't even chosen by the teacher, but was chosen years ago by a coursebook writer who was more preoccupied with illustrating a set of language points than in finding a text that would be of interest to students on any human or intellectual grounds.

We would like to offer you an example of a reading activity that contrasts strongly with the aridity described above. Mario amassed a pile of post over a few days and took these unopened envelopes into class. He explained that he had been very busy and could the students please do the following:

- open his mail for him
- give each item a quick read and write three sentences telling him about the contents
- suggest his proper course of action.

There is nothing complex about the exercise above, but it had the students sitting right on the edge of their chairs. At first they could not believe their eyes or Mario's instructions. The exercise worked because the language student does not come into class expecting this much real life.

The EFL letter-writing community

Over the past few years, we have become aware of a group of teachers who have always used letters with their students. This book is dedicated to them and their students. But who are they? Ms Goethals teaches German in Belgium. When the Berlin Wall came down, her students began to ask her about how people in the eastern part of Germany lived. This prompted her to have a look through a box of her correspondence with a family in East Germany. She picked out the letters that would teach her students most about recent history and East German attitudes, and shared them with her class. She was making good use of a rich source of relevant, person-centered reading comprehension.

A teacher we met at a workshop in Devon had a mother trotting round the globe. She would share with her EFL students her mother's thoughts on how marvellous or awful the local people were. This paralleled some of her students' feelings about the Devonian community they were living in. These maternal letters served as motivating reading comprehension.

Felix Salmon de Garcia, who works in Santander, Spain, uses letters and oral stories as his main teaching medium with 14-year-olds. He gets them to write letters to children in schools in other countries round the Mediterranean. He then uses the foreign children's letters for a system of oblique correction. He has noticed that his pupils are much more likely to put the 's' on the third person singular of the verb if he corrects this feature in Egyptian children's writing than directly in theirs!

Who is this book for?

We have no precisely prescribed audience for this book, though we would say it is not for your beginners class. It deals usefully with all levels above beginners. Below are some of the types of student who have enjoyed and, we think, profited from the activities we describe:

- Students in composition-writing classes. This book offers them a number of innovative frames to get them wanting to communicate on the page.

- Upper secondary groups throughout Europe for whom a 'Life and institutions' component is an important part of their course. Letters put the reader's finger on the pulse of a society in very detailed and special ways. We wish we had been able to work with native letters when we were studying foreign languages.

- Exam classes. More and more exam boards are examining writing ability by means of the letter format, for example the Key English Test (Cambridge), which is designed to assess Waystage (Council of Europe) ability. The description of the written part of the exam stipulates that candidates should be able to produce 'required data in forms, envelopes, etc., simple standard letters, and personal correspondence (simple messages, simple private letters)'. This book could have been designed to prepare students for the KET (though we have to admit it wasn't!). For more ideas for preparing students for exams, see Peter May: *Exam Classes*, also published in this series

- Adult ESL students in English-speaking countries for whom learning to read and write letters is important to living fully in their new environment.

- University classes in countries like Japan where there may be little genuine communication in English. With this kind of group many of the ideas in Section 3 ('Letters across the class') and Section 4 ('Letters out from the class') will prove to be very useful. People in such groups tend to be more proficient at writing than speaking, and it makes good sense to introduce them to communication in the target language via the written form.

How to use this book

This book is designed to help you create a genuine reading and writing culture in your classroom by using letters, both letters which you bring in from outside and those written by and for the students themselves. It is a book of tried and tested ideas, to be dipped into rather than worked through. The division into four sections reflects the types of activity rather than any progression from easy to difficult, though having said that, Sections 1 and 2 might be seen as a kind of progression, for the teacher anyway.

In Section 1, 'Using our letters', you will find a set of activities based on letters of ours which we felt require very specific treatment. These are ready-made lessons, so you don't have the hassle of searching for your own texts. But we hope that when you have used some of our specific lesson plans you may become inspired by your own letters and want to try out some of the activities in Section 2. The possibilities for exploration are endless: they range from highly focused language work to discussion and role-play. The important thing is to let the text itself guide you.

Section 2, 'Using your letters', contains a range of techniques for use with letters from your postbag. Your students know you, not us, and therefore *your* postbag is the relevant one. If you are a native-speaking teacher of English, you are likely to get enough letters you can share without embarrassment in your classes. If you don't, you may well have colleagues who can help out. If you are a non-native-speaking teacher, you may have friends and acquaintances in English-speaking countries who could pass on to you part of their postbag. Your students are going to be a lot more interested in letters that give a portrait of your friends, say in the UK, the USA, or Australia, than they are likely to be in suit-everybody-suit-nobody coursebook texts. You are a living link between them and the people behind the letters. The techniques in Section 2 will get your classes reading, writing, and talking, and, we hope, listening too.

The rest of the book focuses on the students themselves as letter-writers rather than on texts from outside. Section 3, 'Letters across the class', presents a set of activities for getting students to write to each other. These activities extend the normal oral pairwork of the communicative classroom to the process of learning writing. If you do a lot of the sort of writing proposed here, not only do the students get to know each other, but you also create a written culture in your classroom that allows them to evolve a written voice of their own in the target language. The focus of Section 3 is on fluency rather than accuracy. It aims to help your students write more freely, and to motivate them to want to do enough writing to really improve their command of the language. This section lays stress on self-expression and downplays correction. It seems to us that the fear of making mistakes inhibits written even more than oral expression. Here is what a Qatari student had to say about the work of this sort he did:

Third thing about writing letters also, is about my way of producing words. I used to get the meaning in Arabic then translated it into English formulas. By speeding the writing I started thinking in English, producing words in English, feeling about the language. Knowaday I feel the language.

The writer makes mistakes, but his words are from the heart. In fact all the student examples that we have used as illustrations in the book contain inaccuracies, but each of them has a strong personal message to convey. They can be seen as written samples of student 'interlanguage'.

Section 4, 'Letters out from the class', suggests ways you can get students to leap the walls of the classroom and the school and communicate in writing with people anywhere in the world. These ideas are particularly exciting if you have access to fax or e-mail. (The Appendix will provide you with guidance on adapting activities for email use.)

If you find that there are good things for your students in this book, and discover that you enjoy creating a letter reading and writing community in your class, then you will be joining many other language teachers around the world. Creative, humanistic language teaching has already revolutionized some speaking and listening classes. This book invites you to unstopper your students' creativity in reading and writing classes too.

Take care.

Nicky, Peta, Sheila, and Mario

Letters are commonplace enough, yet what splendid things they are! When someone is in a distant province and one is worried about him, and then a letter suddenly arrives, one feels as though one were seeing him face-to-face. Again, it is a great comfort to have expressed one's feelings in a letter, even though one knows it cannot yet have arrived. If letters did not exist, what dark depressions would come over one! When one has been worrying about something and wants to tell a certain person about it, what a relief it is to put it all down in a letter! Still greater is one's joy when a reply arrives. At that moment a letter really seems like an elixir of life!

From the *Pillow Book of Sei Shonagon*

1 Using our letters

In this chapter, we have brought together lesson plans which focus on language areas and skills suggested by specific letters, most of which have come through our own letterboxes. The activities are ready for you to use in class, and in almost all cases the only preparation needed is to photocopy the relevant worksheets at the back of the book and/or to make an overhead transparency.

If you have read the main Introduction to the book, you may wonder why, when we so strongly advocate using *your own* mail in class, that this chapter presents you with lesson plans built around letters of *ours*? There are two reasons for doing this. The first is that we know some of you simply do not have time to go searching for letters to use in class, whatever the creative intentions of our book. In any case, it may be difficult for you to lay hands on appropriate letters in English. The second is that, in offering you ready-made activities, we are suggesting ways in which a particular letter may inspire very focused treatment. Our hope is that this will encourage you to read your own letters with a pedagogical eye and devise appropriate techniques for their handling in class.

The chapter is divided into two sections: 'Using personal letters' and 'Using formal letters'. In the first section, although language study is not neglected, the emphasis is on content. Inevitably, personal letters are concerned with families, friendships, and other topics which will strike chords with students' own personal experience. Perhaps for this reason, we have often found that students read personal letters with particular care. The emphasis in 'Using formal letters' is more on form and appropriacy. However, the letters we have chosen are very different from artificial 'models'. Their idiosyncracies—as well as being entertaining—will help develop students' sensitivity to style and register.

Using personal letters

1.1 Sorry I couldn't say goodbye

LEVEL	**Intermediate and above**
TIME	**30 minutes**

SKILLS

Speaking and reading

OUTLINE

The students have to guess the situation behind a note which the teacher gradually builds up on the board. The teacher helps the students to reassess their conclusions, and to anticipate choices of vocabulary.

PREPARATION

None.

PROCEDURE

1 On one half of the board, copy the pictures, love-hearts, etc. in the note below. Leave room to write the message. Say nothing to the students.

To Pat,
    Sorry I couldn't say goodbye! I didn't even stir this morning when you went to work. Thank you for letting me stay here these past few days.
    Lots of love
    C.   × × ×

2 As you start to write the first sentence, tell the students to start guessing what kind of message is coming.

3 Use the other half of the board to collect facts and possibilities. Write up whatever the students call out, even when it is contradictory. For example, they might suggest that it is a love letter, or even a suicide note.

4 Write the second sentence, leaving a space for the words 'even stir'. Leave a blank for each letter (_ _ _ _   _ _ _ _), and get the students to guess the words by calling out letters until the correct words are in place.

5 Write the third sentence, leaving a space for the words 'letting me' and 'few'. Do as above, getting students to guess the words. Continue to encourage them to guess what kind of letter it is, and write up their ideas on the other half of the board. If necessary, prompt them with questions such as 'How old do you think the writer is?' 'Which sex is the writer?—Why do you think so?' Students should try to give reasons for their suggestions and objections.

6 Add 'Lots of love, C', and get students to come to a final decision about the situation behind the note. Give the answer, which is that is was left by a 16-year-old girl for the mother of one of her friends, at whose house she had been a guest for a few days.

7 Round off the activity with a whole-class discussion. Encourage students to comment on the way the writer's choice of words helped, or hindered, them in guessing the origin of the note. They may also want to comment on its cultural aspects, such as the relationships between teenagers and older people.

COMMENTS   This short text produces lively discussion on language because a lover (as most students assume the writer is) would probably not say 'Thank you for letting me stay', and nor would a family member. Also, a child would be unlikely to use the word 'stir'. Students usually guess, correctly, that the receiver is an adult as they have a job.

1.2 My love life's going like a bomb

LEVEL   **Intermediate and above**

TIME   **45–60 minutes**

SKILLS   **All**

OUTLINE   Students listen to, and then write, a letter from a teenager.

PREPARATION   Make a copy of Worksheet 1.2 (letter from Clara to Kate) for each student, and then one for yourself. If you decide to present the letter in role as the writer, you will also need an envelope.

PROCEDURE   1 Put the following questions on the board:
Am I male or female?
How old am I?
Who am I writing to?
What am I most interested in at the moment?

2 Give out the copies of the letter and ask the students to read it silently. Alternatively, if you enjoy acting, you could pretend to write the letter in role as a 13-year-old girl writing to a female schoolfriend of the same age. Read it out loud to yourself as you write. Repeat sentences as you finish them as though to check them before composing the next one. Read it through at the end without stopping before sealing it in an envelope.

3 When the students have read (and perhaps listened to) the letter, get them to discuss their answers to the questions in pairs. Then have a brief whole-class feedback session.

4 Ask the students to write a letter in role as one of the boys Clara mentions. Monitor and correct their work as they write.

5 Collect in the letters and read some of them out. Ask the group to guess which were written by male, and which by female, members of the class.

1.3 It's a girl

LEVEL	**Intermediate and above**
TIME	**50–60 minutes**
SKILLS	**Reading and speaking**
OUTLINE	Students discuss a photograph and read the letter which accompanies it.
PREPARATION	Make a copy of Worksheet 1.3A (photo of Beatriz) for every three students. Cut the worksheet into sections A and B, as indicated. Make a copy of Worksheet 1.3B (letter from T to Sarah) for each student.
PROCEDURE	**1** Divide the class into groups of three and give out a copy of section A of the photo to each group. Ask the students to guess what the rest of the photo shows. You could prompt them by asking questions such as:

– Do you think the hands are those of a man or a woman?
– What do you think they are holding?

2 Have a brief, whole-class feedback session in which students share their ideas.

3 Give out section B of the photo. Ask the students, again in their groups, questions such as:

– How old do you think the baby is?
– Who do you think is holding the baby?
– Who do you think took the photo?

Ask them to discuss their own feelings about babies. Again, prompt them with questions such as:

– What are the most/least enjoyable things about having a baby?
– How do you think life changes if you have a baby?

4 Give out the copies of Worksheet 1.3B and tell the students to read it silently. Then ask them to decide, in their groups, whether it was written by the baby's father or by her mother.

5 Open the discussion to the whole class and ask the groups to give their reasons for their decision. Tell them that in fact it was Beatriz's father who wrote the letter.

VARIATION

If, at the end of the activity, you feel closer study of the language in the letter would be appropriate, ask the students to underline three expressions that they like and then to paraphrase them. Check the students' work, correcting where necessary.

COMMENTS

Towards the end of the activity, students may find themselves discussing their own understanding of what are typically 'male' and 'female' attitudes: for example, 'Only the mother would write in as much detail about the baby'; 'No, if it was written by the mother she would have written the whole letter about the baby.'

1.4 A letter from Liverpool

LEVEL

Intermediate

TIME

30–40 minutes (more if the reply is to be written in class)

SKILLS

Speaking, reading, and writing

OUTLINE

Students study a personal letter in detail and then write a reply.

PREPARATION

Make one copy of Worksheet 1.4A (letter from Ruth to Sally) and of Worksheet 1.4B for every two students. (If the students are to write their replies as homework, they may each need their own copy of the letter.)

PROCEDURE

1 Introduce the topic of personal letters by asking questions such as:
– Do you receive many personal letters?
– What kinds of things are they usually about?
– How do you feel when an envelope addressed to you arrives and you recognize the handwriting of a friend or a close relative?

2 Ask the students to work in pairs. Hand out copies of Worksheets 1.4A and 1.4B to each pair.

3 Get the students, in their pairs, to read the letter and then work their way through the questions.

4 Check the answers with the whole class.

Answer key
1   bumped into = met unexpectedly
    about to = on the point of (+ -ing)
    hospitable = kind, welcoming
    look after = take care of
    contemporary = modern
    keeping in touch = remaining in contact
    get in touch = make contact

2a In fact they are old friends. A good guess would also be
    relatives of a similar age, for example, sisters or cousins.
2b Reading, perhaps visiting art galleries. (Not travelling,
    since this is her first visit abroad for 10 years!)

3a In return for guiding the Arnhem couple around Liverpool
    city centre.
3b They look after an art gallery.
3c It was the first time she had met victims of modern anti-
    Semitism.

4   She enjoys reading long books.
5   March 1990.

Photocopiable © Oxford University Press

5 Ask the students to reply to this letter, either in class or for
homework. Ask them to imagine that Ruth's letter was written to
them. Tell them to comment on her news, and then add real
news of their own.

6 If possible, allow time for the students to read each others'
answers.

COMMENTS   This activity is useful practice for exam questions in which
candidates are asked to reply to a letter.

1.5 Feeling threatened

LEVEL   **Intermediate and above**

TIME   **30–40 minutes**

SKILLS   **All**

OUTLINE   Students read extracts from a letter and then write the postcard
referred to in it.

PREPARATION   Make one copy of Worksheet 1.5 (extract from a letter to Peta from her mother). If you have an overhead projector, you could prepare a transparency of the postcard text below, but this is not essential. Recall, as vividly as you can, a time when you felt threatened by some kind of public disturbance, for example a fight at a football match or a political demonstration which turned nasty.

PROCEDURE   **1** Tell the students about your experience of feeling threatened. Ask who can bring to mind a situation in which they felt threatened by some kind of public disturbance. Invite them to tell the other students about it (but see Comments below).

2 Ask the students to work in pairs. Give out the copies of Worksheet 1.5 and ask them to read it. Tell them that the letter is from a 67-year-old mother to her 40-year-old daughter.

3 Ask the students, still in their pairs, to write the postcard referred to in the letter.

4 Tell the students to leave their postcard messages on their desks and to go round reading each others'.

5 Either read out the postcard text below, or show it on an overhead projector. Get students to compare their messages with the original.

1.5.92

Darling, am now in Seattle. We had planned to go out this afternoon to the shops but the threat of more riots keeps us in the hotel. So far only peaceful students march but they have closed all the shops. Last night the hooligans were out burning and smashing windows. We leave here early Sunday morning. Have packed!
  Happy birthday!
  Mummy.

Photocopiable © Oxford University Press

COMMENTS   Obviously, in some teaching contexts, it is not wise to raise the topic of political disturbances. In any case, this topic needs to be handled sensitively as some students may have had frightening experiences.

1.6 Idioms galore

LEVEL **Intermediate and above**

TIME **40–50 minutes**

SKILLS **All, but especially reading**

OUTLINE The students study a personal letter for the information it offers about the writer, and its use of idiomatic language.

PREPARATION Make one copy of Worksheet 1.6A (letter from Sue to Glenys and Eddie) and Worksheet 1.6B for each student.

PROCEDURE 1 Hand out both the worksheets. At this stage, do not give the students any background information about the letter.

2 Give the students a few minutes to read the letter for gist, and to write their answers to the first two questions on Worksheet 1.6B.

3 Check these with the whole class (suggested answers below) before asking the students to continue the worksheet.

4 Give the students 10 to 15 minutes to finish the worksheet. Tell them to get into small groups (three to six) to compare their answers. Be on hand to suggest answers when the group is unsure.

5 Ask the students to remain in their groups and, using their intuition as well as the information in the letter, to put together a verbal picture of the writer, her personality, and her family. One member of the group should make brief notes.

6 Invite each group to read out their notes to the rest of the class.

7 Read out the following:

'Sue is an English teacher with a real joie-de-vivre and a good sense of humour. She's in her mid-fifties but looks and sounds much younger. She's a great talker and is always full of anecdotes. She used to teach in Cambridge, but is living in Ethiopia because her husband has a job as an economic adviser there. They've got two grown-up children, both born in Israel, one living in Canada and the other in England.'

8 The class decides which group's description is closest to the one above.

Answer key

1   Ethiopia

2   To tell them how thrilled she was to hear her friends on radio, and to ask them a favour.

3   Ten days

4a 'mail'; 'stores'
 b 'famil<u>air</u>'; 'an<u>d</u> export promotion'

5   She is reminding Eddie to order exemption forms from the local VAT* office. Non-residents who buy products in Britain and take them back to their own countries can claim back the VAT they have paid on the product.

   * VAT (Value Added Tax) is a European purchase tax.

6   Answers to this question will obviously vary, but have some non-idiomatic 'translations' ready just in case, for example:
 a I was really surprised
 b While drinking/enjoying a cup of tea
 c to write to you
 d not wanting to appear inferior
 e which was the reason for
 f delighted
 g never have them available
 h taking care of/checking on

7   The delay in naming the subject of the sentence adds drama and suspense. This is a fairly common rhetorical device.

8   'Came forth' is Biblical English for 'came out'. Sue uses it here to make the story sound dramatic.

9   Sue uses exclamation marks not only to signal surprise (the first 2 sentences; the comment in brackets about Ben Bardan), but also to emphasize her ironic statement about the length of time Ben appeared on the screen.

VARIATION

If you decide to use one of your own personal letters, you may be able to pre-record a description of the writer and their family made by a mutual friend. In this case, you can play it to your students at step 7.

COMMENTS

When choosing letters of your own for this kind of treatment, look for a text which offers plenty of clues about the writer and has good potential for language work. For example, it could contain several idioms and phrasal verbs, and/or an interesting variety and use of tenses.

1.7 Is this man safe to be let out?

LEVEL   **Advanced**

TIME   **50–75 minutes**

SKILLS   **All**

OUTLINE   Students exchange reactions to a picture and write a letter.

PREPARATION   Make copies of Worksheet 1.7A (the Artist's Christmas card), one for every two students. Make a copy of Worksheet 1.7B (the Artist's story) for each student.

PROCEDURE   1 Ask the students to work in pairs. Without saying anything, give a copy of Worksheet 1.7A to each pair. Give the students time to look at it carefully and to exchange reactions.

2 Ask 'Where do you think the picture comes from?' Possible answers are:
– a comic strip
– a telephone-pad doodle
– the cover of a science-fiction novel.
Encourage imaginative suggestions.

3 Ask the students, still in their pairs, to list:
– any *facts* they can discover about the artist from the card
– any things they think are *probable* about the artist
– any fantastic *possibilities* that occur to them.

4 Put three headings on the board: Facts; Probabilities; Possibilities. Ask the students for their ideas and list them.
Tell the students that the picture is a Christmas card sent by a man to his doctor.

5 Give out the copies of Worksheet 1.7B and ask the students to read it silently.

6 Ask them, working individually, to write a letter either to the man or to his doctor, saying whether or not they think the card he designed and made is an indication of insanity. Ask them to give reasons, and to make their own analysis of the symbolism.

7 Allow time for students to read each others' letters.

VARIATION   Step 6 could be done as homework.

COMMENTS   This activity may well lead to discussion about what is 'normal' and what is 'mad' behaviour.

Using formal letters

1.8 Analysing a formal letter structure

LEVEL	**Intermediate**
TIME	**45–60 minutes**
SKILLS	**All**
OUTLINE	Students reconstruct a formal letter which is dictated to them. They learn, or revise, formulas which are frequently used in formal letters.
PREPARATION	Make one copy of Worksheet 1.8 (letter from Susan Woolfe to Ms Sanderson) for each student. Alternatively, copy the letter onto an overhead projector transparency. Prepare eight 3cm-wide strips of blank paper for each student.
PROCEDURE	1 Give out eight strips of blank paper to each student. Tell them that you are going to dictate six sentences, and that they should write each one on a separate slip of paper. Dictate the following sentences, leaving out the underlined words and telling students to put a dash where they occur.

a Dear Ms Sanderson
b On your first morning, I <u>suggest</u> you arrive at 9.30 a.m.
c Please could you sign the second copy and <u>return</u> it to me.
d <u>Please</u> go to Main Reception and ask for me.
e Following our recent interviews, I am pleased to offer you the <u>position</u> of Copywriter in our Publicity Department.
f A Contract of Employment with details of terms and conditions is <u>enclosed</u>.

2 Put the students into groups of three or four and ask them to:

– guess what type of text these sentences come from
– guess what words fill the blanks
– put the sentences in the correct order
– suggest a formula for signing off at the end and write it on one of their two remaining blank slips.

3 Ask the students if they think anything is missing from the letter. Dictate this sentence, asking students to write it on their remaining blank slip:

g As we agreed, you will start on 1st June.

Tell the students to add it to their ordered sentences in an appropriate place.

4 Give out the worksheets, or display the original text on an overhead projector. Tell the students to check their work against it. Explain any words and expressions which are still causing problems, and discuss any alternatives to the order of the sentences in the original text (e.g. it would be possible to put 'As we agreed, you will start on 1st June' at the beginning of the final paragraph).

COMMENTS

This activity is good practice for writing formal letters in examinations because it requires students to study the structure and language of this kind of letter in some detail.

1.9 Thank you

LEVEL

Intermediate and above

TIME

40–60 minutes

SKILLS

All

OUTLINE

Students study the language in a formal letter of thanks, and write their own.

PREPARATION

Make one copy of Worksheet 1.9 (letter from Carol Miller to Julie and Rob) for each student. Make an extra copy, enlarged if possible, for every four students. Cut these extra copies into single-line strips and keep them in sets.

PROCEDURE

1 Divide the class into groups of four. Hand out one set of strips to each group and ask students to organize them into a formal letter of thanks.

2 Hand out copies of the complete letter so that the group can check their organization of the strips.

3 Stress that this is a typical formal letter of thanks which the writer has tried to personalize by the use of first names, resulting in rather an odd juxtaposition of styles. Ask the students, working individually, to underline the words, phrases, or sentences which seem to them to produce the formal style, and then to compare their choices with another student's.

4 Draw a line down the middle of the board. On one side, collect the formal expressions which the students have underlined. The collection should look something like this:

I would like to take this opportunity ...
... on behalf of ...
social committee   performing
musical evening
... would have been deprived ...
... thoroughly enjoyable social event
... do us the honour ...
social functions
... please do not hesitate to contact ...

5 Ask the students to think of situations in which they have had to write a formal letter of thanks. List these on the other side of the board.

6 Ask students to choose one of the situations on the board and to write a formal letter of thanks. Tell them to use formal words and expressions from the original letter where appropriate.

7 If there is time at the end of the lesson, get the students to put their letters up on the wall so they can read each others'. Afterwards, collect in the letters for correction.

1.10 Spoof correspondence

LEVEL	**Intermediate and above**
TIME	**30–45 minutes**
SKILLS	**Reading and speaking**
OUTLINE	Students read two formal letters, one a reply to the other. They study the formal language in both letters, and comment on some unusual features in the second letter.
PREPARATION	Make one copy of Worksheet 1.10A (letter from Peter Thomas to the Marketing Manager) and one copy of Worksheet 1.10B (letter from the Public Relations Officer to Peter Thomas) for each student.
PROCEDURE	1 Ask the students the following questions:

- What is the average annual mileage for a private car? (About 10,000 miles/16,000 kilometres in the UK.)
- How long does a set of tyres normally last? (About 30,000 miles/48,000 kilometres.)

– How many miles/kilometres would you expect the average
engine to run without giving major problems? (About 80,000
miles/128,000 kilometres.)
– How often would you expect the average owner to change car?
(About every three years in the UK.)
– In your country, do people ever refer to their cars as if they
were people?

2 Hand out the copies of Worksheet 1.10A. Tell the students
that Peter Thomas actually sent this letter. Ask the students to
read it and, in pairs, to underline any expressions which they
think are typical of a formal letter in English. Ask them, too, to
list the ways in which the format of a formal letter differs from
that of a personal letter.

3 Draw a line down the middle of the board. On one side, write
up the formal expressions which the students have noted. On the
other, list the ways in which the format of a formal letter differs
from that of a personal letter.

The list of formal expressions should look something like this:
I am writing to complain about ...
We are having to consider (do)ing ...
(The tyres) in question ...
... something in excess of ...
Could you suggest ... ?
... perhaps some financial advantage to ourselves ...
... to offset ...
... we will no doubt ...

The characteristic format of a formal letter is:
– Writer's address in top right-hand corner
– Date either below writer's address or above addressee's
– Addressee's name and address below writer's address, but to
the left
– Letter begins 'Dear Sir/Madam', unless the writer knows the
name of the person they are writing to
– Letter ends 'Yours faithfully', unless the writer knows the
name of the person they are writing to, in which case it ends
'Yours sincerely'.

4 Ask the students to get into groups of three or four and to
decide on:
– Peter Thomas' purpose in writing the letter
– Whether they think the Marketing Manager replied, and if so,
how.

5 Have a brief, whole-class feedback session.

6 Hand out copies of the company's reply to Mr Thomas. Ask
the students to read it and, as they did with the first letter, to
underline any expressions typical of an ordinary formal letter.
Add these to the list of formal expressions already on the board.

They include:
With reference to your letter dated ...
... we are sorry to hear ...
... we feel sure that ...
We look forward to ...

You could also ask a more advanced class to comment on:
- the expressions in which the Public Relations Officer has taken up Peter Thomas' idea of writing about the car as if it was a living creature
- examples of language used in an exaggeratedly formal way for humorous effect.

COMMENTS

This is a particularly useful exercise to do with classes preparing for examinations which require formal letter-writing skills, for example the FCE, CAE, and CPE. We have found that students enjoy reading authentic texts which play with formal English in a humorous way. Their laughter helps to diminish any anxiety they may have about the formal language.

1.11 A final demand

LEVEL

Advanced

TIME

45 minutes

SKILLS

Writing and reading

OUTLINE

Students write a final demand letter, and then analyse the grammar, syntax, and choice of words in an authentic example.

PREPARATION

Make one copy of Worksheet 1.11 (final demand from Beale's Bookshop) for each student.

PROCEDURE

1 Ask the students to work in pairs. Tell them that they work for a large bookshop. They have a customer who has an account. One letter has already been sent reminding the customer to pay his account, but they have had no response. They must now, in their pairs, compose a final demand letter of no more than five sentences. Monitor the students' writing, correcting and offering help where necessary.

2 When they have finished, ask them to leave their letters on their desks. Give them five or ten minutes to walk around the room and read as many of the other students' letters as possible.

3 Give out the copies of the letter that was actually sent. Tell the students to read it carefully. Ask them the following questions.

a What is the aim of this letter?

b How many examples of 'we' and 'our' can you spot? Why does the individual writer of the letter use the plural form?

c (1) How many examples of 'you' and 'your' can you find? (2) Pick out the passives.

d Find all the words and phrases expressing sadness and unwillingness.

e Which words are connected with the notion of time? Why are so many used?

f What does the writer mean by 'further steps'?

Tell the students to work their way through the questions in pairs, and then to compare their answers with another pair.

3 Check the answers with the whole class.

Answer key (and commentary)

a To jolt or scare the addressee into paying his/her account.

b There are four examples of 'we' and two of 'our'. The first person plural indicates that the employee of Beale's Bookshop who has signed the letter is acting on behalf of the company, not as an individual. It also expresses an authoritative stance: 'we' (plural) against 'you' (singular).

c (1) Apart from the formula 'Yours faithfully', there is only one 'you' and one 'your'.

    (2) There are three examples of the passive. The British way of threatening tends to be impersonal.

d A common way of inducing a feeling of guilt in someone else is to declare the deep sadness they have caused you by their behaviour. This letter uses this technique heavily: for example, 'We are disappointed'; 'we are reluctant'; 'we shall be forced'; 'regrettably'.

e 'Previous'; 'overdue'; 'immediate'; 'now'; 'further'; 'by return'; 'temporarily'; 'pending'. These repeated references emphasize that Beale's Bookshop are concerned with time as much as with money.

f An obvious further step would be prosecution in a court of law. To allude to this is much more threatening than to state it directly.

---

4 Ask your students to look again at the letters they wrote, and ask them:

– How many passives did you use?
– Could you change any of your active sentences into passives to make the letter feel more formal?
– Did you include any of the features in the sample letter that we have just discussed?

1.12 Don't be duped!

LEVEL

Advanced

TIME

45–75 minutes (or 45 minutes plus homework)

SKILLS

All

OUTLINE

Students analyse an item of direct mail advertising and then the text of an advertisement.

PREPARATION

Make one copy of Worksheet 1.12 (Christmas Shopping letter) for each student. Take some adverts from magazines and newspapers in English. There should be at least one for each student in your class.

PROCEDURE

1 Ask the students 'Do you enjoy shopping for presents? Why/ Why not?' Make two headings on the board, 'Why?' and 'Why not?', and list the students' ideas. Ask the students when they give presents in their cultures, for example, birthdays, name days, Christmas, or Eid ul-Fitr (the end of Ramadan).

2 Give out the copies of 1.12A. Ask the students to read it through quickly and to check any unfamiliar vocabulary in their dictionaries.

3 Ask the students to identify three expressions in the letter that tell them it is an advertisement. (Likely answers include 'Two Free Gifts'; 'do all your shopping with us'; 'Spend £50 or more ...'.)

4 Get students to comment on the ways in which advertising copywriters try and persuade potential customers to buy a product. Invite any students who have had experience of writing advertising copy to tell the rest of the class about it.

5 Write the following characteristics of advertiser's language on the board, or display them on an overhead projector:
- *personalization*: creating the illusion of familiarity between writer and reader
- *empathy*: assuming the reader feels the same way as the writer
- *reinforcement*: making the reader remember a message by constant repetition
- *positive language:* using plenty of superlatives, and words and phrases with positive associations.

Ask the students, working in pairs, to find examples of each of these in the letter.

6 Get the pairs to join into groups of four and compare their examples.

7 Go through the devices with the whole class, eliciting examples.

8 Put out the adverts you have taken from magazines. Ask the students to choose one each. Tell them, working on their own, to find examples of copywriter's devices as they did with the letter. If they find devices which are not in the list, tell them to describe them.

9 Ask them to write a brief analysis of the advertisement.

10 Ask the students to put up their advertisements on the wall, with their analyses beside them. Give them time to go round looking at each others' analyses.

VARIATION   Steps 8 and 9 can be done for homework.

1.13 Who reads *The Economist*?

LEVEL   **Intermediate and above**

TIME   **90 minutes**

SKILLS   **All**

OUTLINE   Students write a promotional letter for a magazine, and then study a letter actually sent out by the magazine, paying particular attention to its style and register.

PREPARATION   Make one copy of Worksheet 1.13A (information about *The Economist*) and Worksheet 1.13B (letter from *The Economist*) for every two students.

PROCEDURE

1 If you have a copy of *The Economist* available, show it to the class and ask:

– Do any of you read this magazine?
– Who do you think it is designed for?
– What kind of articles would you expect to find in it?

If you do not have a copy available, explain that *The Economist* is a weekly magazine aimed at people who are involved in the running of businesses.

2 Ask the students to get into groups of three or four. Explain that they are a marketing team for the magazine. Their brief is to write a letter to potential new customers encouraging them to subscribe to it.

3 Hand out copies of Worksheet 1.13A. Tell the students that they need not use all the information in their letter, but can make a selection of the points they think are the most important.

4 Tell the students to write their letters in their groups. When they have finished, get them to leave them out on their desks or put them up on the walls. They can then walk around and read the other groups' letters, and select the one they would send if they were running the advertising campaign and had to make a final decision.

5 Ask individual students to tell the rest of the class about their final decisions, and their reasons for them.

6 Dictate the phrases below. (They are all from the 'Letter from *The Economist*', but do not tell the students this.) As they write down each one, tell the students to indicate who they think the addressee could be: an academic, a friend, or a business person? (To save time, tell them to write 'A', 'F', or 'BP' beside each phrase.)

Phrases for dictation:

a Who doesn't read *The Economist*?
b everyday folk
c to be perfectly frank
d Four out of five subscribers renew every year.
e leading articles on the key developments in politics, trade, economics, and culture throughout the world
f There's nothing quite like it.
g these highly advantageous terms are offered
h I can assure you that you'll be in very good, if select, company.

7 Tell students, in pairs, to compare their versions of the dictated sentences, checking grammar and spelling. They should also discuss the possible addressees.

8 Hand out Worksheet 1.13B. The students can now check the dictated phrases and compare the original letter to their own. If the students have enjoyed the lesson, this step may well develop into a discussion about style, register, and the language used in advertising.

2 Using your letters

In this chapter, we introduce techniques which you can use with items of mail that come through your own letterbox. It goes without saying that using your own letters, or those of friends and colleagues, will add a new dimension to your lessons. The most well-worn of techniques like dictation, reading comprehension, or translation will come alive for the students if the material is a real piece of communication addressed to *their* teacher. For example, in 2.1, 'Getting to know you', you introduce yourself to a new class by presenting them with a message, or part of a letter, which gives the students some clues about you. They discuss what the message tells them about you and then use it as the basis for questions. The information in the message gives the students a starting point for their questions, and is much more motivating than 'So, what would you like to ask me about?'

For students in 'Culture and institutions' classes, letter texts can provide a rich source of information about the target culture. Indeed, in our experience, students often learn more about a foreign country from the most unpromising of texts, for example a reminder from the library, a delivery note, or a message to the milkman, than they do from conventional sources. If you, or people you know, are the recipients of the correspondence used in class, so much the better: students can put the texts in the context of real peoples' lives rather than of some imaginary cultural stereotype. Many ELT examinations test students' writing ability with tasks in which they are required to write notes or letters. Items from your own mailbag, or of your own choice, can offer much more interesting models for exam classes than coursebook texts do.

Published letters in English, written by famous — or not-so-famous — people, offer an alternative to your own correspondence, and are of particular interest for those of you who may have problems in getting hold of enough items of mail in English to use in class. We have included two activities here in which we have used published letters, and there is a list of books of letters on page 129.

This chapter is divided into three sections, 'Using texts intact', 'Changing the text', and 'Text as springboard'. Many of the activities are illustrated with example texts. Obviously, as we have argued above, it is better if you can find your own texts, but if this proves impossible and the texts we have chosen are suitable for your class, you could use them instead.

Using texts intact

2.1 Getting to know you

LEVEL	**Elementary and above**
TIME	**40–50 minutes**
SKILLS	**All**
OUTLINE	Students get to know the teacher and each other by sharing notes or extracts from personal letters. The teacher provides an authentic example, and the students invent their own.
PREPARATION	Choose a typical note, like the one below, left for you by someone in your household, or from a neighbour. It should contain clues to your lifestyle. Alternatively, select a brief extract from a personal letter which you do not mind sharing with the class.

> Mum. Can you pick us up (me + 3) from the Sports Centre after your dance class? Don't worry we'll get ourselves s/th if you're working this evening. Tizzy said she'd get bread, milk etc in town. See you later – Jo

Photocopiable © Oxford University Press

PROCEDURE

1 Write the note on the board, or show it on an overhead projector.

2 Ask the students to discuss in pairs what they learn from the note about you and your lifestyle.

3 After they have told you what they have learnt, invite them to ask you questions about yourself which may, but need not necessarily, be based on evidence in the note.

4 Answer their questions, asking some open ones in return such as 'Does anyone else … ?'

5 Ask the students to invent a typical note that they might easily have received from a member of their household or from a neighbour or colleague. Tell them to be prepared to answer questions.

6 The students then present their notes to the whole class, as you did. In larger classes, students can work in pairs or small groups, and then share things they have learnt about other students with the rest of the class.

7 Collect in the notes for correction.

COMMENTS

1 This activity is particularly useful near the start of a course, but can work well at any stage.

2 It is good practice for the Oxford Preliminary Exam, in which there is often a question on message writing.

Acknowledgements

This activity is adapted from one used by John Barnett.

2.2 Talking about postcards

LEVEL

Intermediate and above

TIME

50–60 minutes

SKILLS

Speaking, listening, and reading

OUTLINE

Students talk about their personal attitudes to sending and receiving postcards. They then read and discuss a set of postcards.

PREPARATION

Copy Worksheet 2.2A ('Sending postcards' questionnaire) for half the class and Worksheet 2.2B ('Receiving postcards' questionnaire) for the other half. Collect a set of about five postcards for each group of six to twelve students.

PROCEDURE

1 Divide the students into even-numbered groups of, ideally, between six and twelve. Give half of each group Worksheet 2.2A and the other half Worksheet 2.2B.

2 Tell the students to work their way through the questionnaires individually, answering in note form.

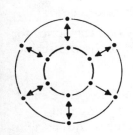

3 Organize each group so that they are standing or sitting in two circles, inner and outer, divided according to which questionnaire they have answered. The people on the inside face those on the outside (what Friederike Klippel calls 'the onion').

(from Friederike Klippel: *Keep Talking*)

4 In turn, each student reads out their question 1 to their partner and they both talk about their answers. They must stick to the subject of the two question 1s until you give the sign for the outer circle to move round one place in a clockwise direction. Then they start discussing their answers to their question 2s with a new partner. Repeat until all the questions have been covered.

5 Hand out the sets of postcards, one set for each group. While the students are reading them, write up, or display on an overhead projector, some questions for the groups to discuss. Here are a few suggestions:

- Which picture do you find the most attractive?
- Is each text connected with its picture and, if so, how?
- Which handwriting do you like best, and what do you like about it?
- Which is the best-written card (in terms of composition, not handwriting)?
- Which card would you most like to have received?
- Find one phrase in each card that you would have written differently.

6 Give the groups about 10 minutes to discuss the questions, and then bring them together for a brief whole-class feedback session.

2.3 Postcards to one family

LEVEL

Intermediate and above

TIME

50–60 minutes

SKILLS

Reading, speaking, and writing

OUTLINE

Students build up a picture of one family from a set of postcards. They then write to the family asking nosy questions.

PREPARATION

Collect about five postcards addressed to one family. Photocopy the texts once for each group of five students in your class.

Type out the handwritten texts and photocopy one transcript for each group. Alternatively, make a transparency of the transcript and use an overhead projector.

PROCEDURE

1 Divide the class into groups of about five students. Give each group copies of the handwritten texts. If you are using real postcards, you could show the students the pictures and, as a warm-up activity, ask them to try and match the pictures to the texts.

2 Ask the students to transcribe the texts as accurately as possible, including the mistakes made by the original writers. Encourage guesswork if necessary.

3 Give out the typed transcripts. Get the students to check their own transcripts against these.

4 Ask the group members to take turns reading out the texts to one another, gradually building up a picture of the family. Ask them to start with the facts and then 'read between the lines' more imaginatively.

5 Ask each student to find a partner from a different group. Tell the pairs to discuss ways in which the family is different from, or similar to, their own. Ask them to consider whether their own family would get on well with the postcard family.

6 Ask the students, either individually or in their pairs, to write a letter to a member of the postcard family asking them personal questions. Tell them they can be as nosy as they like!

7 If there is time, one partner in each pair can respond to the letter orally, in role as a family member.

VARIATION   After step 3, ask the students to identify as many spelling, grammar, and punctuation mistakes in the original texts as they can in 10 minutes. With a teenage class, this might take the form of a competition among groups.

2.4 Official correspondence

LEVEL   **Intermediate and above**

TIME   **60 minutes**

SKILLS   **All**

OUTLINE   Students read a variety of official correspondence which introduces aspects of the target culture.

PREPARATION   Collect some official correspondence from two or three families who you know, and who live in the target culture: for example, letters from clubs they belong to, reminders of appointments with the dentist or optician, even old gas bills. Explain how you are going to use them and make sure they are happy for all the items to be used in class. Photocopy one complete set per five or six students in your class. Prepare a list of the types of correspondence in the set (see the example below) for putting up on the board or on an overhead projector. For example, your collection might include the following:

- a reminder from the doctor about an injection
- an appointment for a driving test
- an appeal for funds from a school or college
- a reminder from the Electricity Company about an unpaid bill
- details of membership of a health/music/art/sports, etc. club
- notification about local taxes for the coming year
- a bill for fitting a cat-flap in the front door

PROCEDURE

1 Divide the class into groups of five or six students. Give out one copy of the set of correspondence to each group. Ask the students to decide how many families are being addressed, and which family received which mail. This is an easy task which introduces students gently to reading the sometimes difficult texts.

2 Check that the groups have correctly identified which items of correspondence belong to which families.

3 Write up, or display, the list of correspondence and ask the students to match each item with its description.

4 Ask the students, in their groups, to build up a 'fact file' for each family, based on the information in the correspondence. For example, the fact file for one family, the Burtons, might look like this:

> Burton
> A member of the family has been learning to drive
> A member of the family is thinking of joining a tennis club
> They have at least one cat

Photocopiable © Oxford University Press

5 Have a brief, whole-class session in which groups compare their fact files.

6 Ask the students, still in their groups, to discuss what they have learnt about the target culture from the correspondence they have been studying. Ask them, too, to say in what ways their own cultures are similar, or different.

7 Bring the groups together again for a whole-class feedback session.

COMMENTS

This activity grew out of a comment made by an English-speaking student of French that he would 'dearly love to study a French telephone bill!'

Changing the text

2.5 Simplification

LEVEL   **Intermediate and above**

TIME   **30 minutes**

SKILLS   **All**

OUTLINE   Students summarize a formal letter for an imaginary 10-year-old.

PREPARATION   Find and copy four formal letters, enough of each for a quarter of the class. These could be business letters, or perhaps letters from clubs and societies.

PROCEDURE   1 Divide the class into four groups. Give each group copies of one of the four formal letters. Tell them they are to read the letter and agree in their group on a summary of five sentences or fewer which would be understood by a 10-year-old child. Stress that a 10-year-old must understand it.

2 Think yourself into the role of a 10-year-old.

3 Each group reads you their summary and, in role as a child, you question everything you don't understand. (This phase can produce hilarious results!)

4 Put up copies of the four letters so that the students can walk round and compare the summaries they have just heard with the original texts.

Acknowledgements
We first saw this idea used in Tom Hinton's class in Tokyo.

2.6 Doctored texts

LEVEL   **Advanced**

TIME   **Up to 60 minutes, depending on the length of the text**

SKILLS   **All**

OUTLINE   Students try to spot the alterations in part of a letter, correct them, and do their own doctored version of the other part.

PREPARATION

Choose a letter which will lend itself to being altered in an amusing way. An advertising letter (see Worksheet 2.6) works particularly well, but you might find that doctoring a very formal letter or one with a threatening tone, for example, produces the result you want. Leave the first half of the letter untouched, but change words or phrases in the second half to completely alter the meaning. Type out your doctored version (and the original letter too if it is on headed notepaper and needs to be disguised). Photocopy one doctored text and one original letter per student.

PROCEDURE

1 Hand out copies of the doctored letter and get the students to read it silently. They will eventually realize there is something wrong. Ask them to 'correct' it individually.

2 Tell the students to compare their corrections in groups of three or four.

3 Hand out copies of the original letter and give the students time to read it and compare it with their own corrected versions.

4 Now ask the students, working individually, to alter the first half of the text. Tell them to change words or phrases without making the text ungrammatical.

5 The students read each others' letters and comment on the changes they like best.

COMMENTS

This technique demands very close reading from the students. Interestingly, some students seem to prefer doctoring the original text, while others are happier reinstating it.

Acknowledgements

This is an extension of an idea in *Vocabulary* by John Morgan and Mario Rinvolucri, published in this series.

2.7 Letter transformation

LEVEL

Intermediate

TIME

15–20 minutes in lesson 1
10–15 minutes in lesson 2

SKILLS

All

OUTLINE

Students play the role of examiners, deleting grammar markers from sentences. A week later they role-play exam candidates, and put the grammar back in.

PREPARATION

Select a short, grammatically correct letter and make one copy per student. Our example below is taken from *A Particular Friendship*, a book of letters written by Dirk Bogarde.

The House
March 5th, 1967

Dear Mrs X,

Thank you so much for your long and charming letter of February 27th enclosing the photographs of the house as it was when you lived here in the thirties. I was tremendously interested and will reply again in a day or two, when I shall have a little more time, and hope to be able to answer some of the questions which you ask. Meanwhile excuse this hurried note: I have been away for a time and there is a large backlog to catch up on.

Sincerely
Dirk Bogarde

The House
March 5th, 1967

Dear Mrs X,

Thank you so much / your long / charming letter / February 27th / (enclose) / photographs / house / it / (be) / when you / (live) / here / thirties. I / (be) / tremendously interested / (reply) / again / day / two, when I (have) / little more time, / (hope) (be able) (answer) / some / questions which you / (ask). Meanwhile / (excuse) / this hurried note: I (be) / away / time / there / (be) / large backlog / (catch up on).

Sincerely
Dirk Bogarde

PROCEDURE

Lesson 1

1 Give the students any background information to the letter which you think might be helpful. With our example text we told the students that the letter was written by the film actor, Dirk Bogarde, to a woman he did not know, but who had lived in his house 30 years before.

2 Hand out the copies of the letter and remind the students that, in examinations, candidates are often asked to turn incomplete sentences like 'I/love/walk/Cambridge/when/pour/rain' into complete grammatical sentences.

3 Ask them to play the part of examiners and delete some of the grammar markers from the letter. For example, we have deleted the articles, conjunctions, and prepositions from Dirk Bogarde's letter, and put the verbs into the infinitive. Ask them to work in twos to write out a copy of their skeleton letter. Tell them to use slashes to indicate where things have been left out. Take in both the original letter and the students' versions.

Lesson 2

4 A few days later, give the students back their skeleton letters and tell them to reconstruct the original.

5 Give out copies of the original letter so that they can check their work.

2.8 Text reconstruction

LEVEL	**All**
TIME	**30–40 minutes**
SKILLS	**Speaking, listening, writing**
OUTLINE	Students reconstruct a text.
PREPARATION	Find two short messages or postcard texts of suitable difficulty for your students (two elementary, two intermediate, and two advanced level texts appear below). Make enough copies for half of your class to work in pairs on one text, and half to work in pairs on the other.

Elementary

Text 1
Mum, I've gone to Sandra's. I'll be back soon. Love, Anna
Text 2
Rob, Sam phoned. Please ring him after six o'clock. Mum

Intermediate

Text 1
Dear Grandad, We're having a wonderful time. The food is excellent and the sun shines every day! Love from all of us.
Text 2
Mum, I've taken the alarm clock. I hope you don't mind. I'll wake you up at seven. See you in the morning, Jo

Advanced

Text 1

Dear Mrs Smith, I have tried to phone Sally several times but there has been no reply. If she fails to return to school, a court warning letter will be issued.
Sue Branston (Education Welfare Officer)

Text 2

Dear Everybody, Here's our new address. After much searching we've finally found a house we both liked and could afford. Time to put roots down. All the best for the coming year, A and S.

PROCEDURE

1 Ask the students to get into pairs. Give out copies of one text to half of the class and the other text to the other half.

2 Ask the pairs to list all the words in their text alphabetically. Advise them to be systematic so they do not miss out any words. For example, Text 1 would look like this:

Anna
back
be
gone
I'll
I've
love
Mum
Sandra's
soon
to

3 Ask the students to exchange their lists, but not their texts, with a pair from the other half of the class.

4 Explain that they must try to reconstruct the original text from the alphabetical lists, but that they can first ask the other pair six questions about the text.

5 Give the pairs a few minutes to prepare their questions.

6 In turn, each pair asks their questions and the other pair answers.

7 Tell each pair to try and reconstruct their text from the word list. They should then check their version against the original text.

2.9 Verb-phrase skeletons

LEVEL	**Intermediate and above**
TIME	**40–50 minutes**
SKILLS	**Reading, writing**
OUTLINE	Students write a letter of a particular genre, basing it on the verbs and verb phrases of an unseen original.
PREPARATION	Select two short letters of the same genre, for example thank-you letters or letters of invitation. They should be about the same length. Make enough copies of one letter for half of the class, and of the other letter for the other half.
PROCEDURE	1 Give half the class copies of one letter and the other half copies of the other. Ask the students, working on their own, to list in order of occurrence all the verbs and verb phrases in their letters. Also ask them to list, on the same sheet of paper, the noun-phrases which give the content of the letter, but this time in jumbled order (see the examples below). Go round checking the students' lists.

Dear Parents and Friends,

I am writing with an invitation to our annual Mothering Sunday Service at St John's Church, New Hinksey on Sunday 26th March at 6.30 p.m. We are also inviting the Scouts to join us and to take part in this Service. We very much hope that you will be able to come.

Yours sincerely,

Helen Alexander

Vicar

I am writing
We are also inviting
to join
to take part
We very much hope
You will be able to come

6.30 p.m.
the Scouts
an invitation to our annual Mothering Sunday Service
St John's Church, New Hinksey
Sunday 26th March

Dear Mr Renfrew,

I am writing to invite you to take part in a panel discussion on: 'Preserving our local Rights of Way' to be held at the Community Centre on 24th March, at 6.30p.m. I also plan to invite a representative from Dudley Park Estate, a local farmer, and probably someone from the Ramblers Association. I do hope you will be able to take part.

Yours sincerely

Miles Mendry

I am writing to invite you
to take part
to be held
I also plan to invite
I do hope
you will be able to take part

6.30 p.m.
'Preserving our local Rights of Way'
24th March
someone from the Rambler's Association
Community Centre
a representative from Dudley Park Estate
a local farmer
a panel discussion

2 Ask the students who have been working on one letter to find partners who have been working on the other. Tell them to swap their verb- and noun-phrase lists, but not their letters.

3 Ask the students, either working on their own or in small groups, to try and reconstruct the original letters from the lists. Tell the class that the two letters are of the same sort.

4 Tell the students to pair up again with the students with whom they swapped verb-phrase lists. They compare their respective reconstructed versions with the two originals.

Acknowledgements

We learnt this technique from Marcial Boo at a Pilgrims technical evening in Summer 1993.

2.10 Skim-reading

LEVEL

Intermediate and above

TIME

50–60 minutes

SKILLS

Skim-reading, writing

OUTLINE

Students skim-read a letter, reorder phrases from it, and respond to it in writing.

PREPARATION

Select a letter with strong personal, political, or emotional content, and on a topic that will interest your students (see the example in Worksheet 2.10). Make a copy for each student, plus a few extra copies for step 1. Take 10 to 12 sentence fragments from the letter and write these in jumbled order—like those below the sample letter—on a separate sheet of paper. Make one copy for every two students, plus some extra copies.

PROCEDURE

1 When all your students have arrived for the lesson, put up several copies of the letter on the walls of the corridor outside the classroom.

2 Ask the students to go outside the classroom. Tell them they will find copies of a letter put up on the walls. Give them an exact amount of time in which to skim-read the letter. (We allowed an advanced class two minutes to read the letter from Harry Truman.)

3 Bring the students back into the classroom and give them the sentence fragments sheet, one between two. Ask them to number the phrases in order of their occurrence in the letter.

4 Check with the whole class that they have ordered the sentences correctly.

5 Give each student a copy of the letter to read at their own speed. Ask them to write up words or phrases they do not understand on the board. Elicit explanations of these from other students, or clear up problems yourself.

6 Ask the students to write an individual response to the letter, either in role as the recipient, or as themselves.

7 Allow time for the students to read each other's letters.

Reply from a student writing as herself:

7th, November

Dear Harry

I don't know what the war is. I only know that the war is a terrible, awful thing. But it <u>can't know reality of the war</u>. I want peace same as you.

As a bomb was dropped in Hiroshima, many people are still suffering from deseases now. I haven't seen these people, but I saw some books and television about them.

Some people have no arm or leg, some people have problem on thier bones. It is difficult to see them, because they are so miserable. We must not start any war again. But war is happening still now. When I was in Japan, I am not interested in war or the incidents which is happening in other country very much. I just thought it was terrible. Since I came to England, I became friends with many people of different nationality. I came to feel that war or other incidents is happening around me. We are human being, so we will die someday or other. But it is stupid idea to hasten our death by war. Do you think so? I hope you make approaches to prevent war as the head.

Yours

Reply from student writing in role as Truman's daughter, Margie:

Dear Daddy,

Mum gave me your letter. It is the first letter for months.

I hope you will come back soon. I miss you so. Every evening I feel so sad, because you don't give me a good-night-kiss. It is not the same when mum tells me a bedtime story.

Mum said, you had a very important job in Berlin for the whole world to do. Why is Berlin so far away? I hope the horrible war will end soon. I hope you are back next week, because I have my summer holiday. I want to go with you and mum to the seaside to build a sand castle on the beach.

Please come back from this bad place Berlin

Margie

| COMMENTS | Reading quickly is a skill that students need to acquire in order to enjoy newspapers and books in English, and for examinations. This activity encourages them to retain not just content but language items as well. |

Text as springboard

2.11 Doodlers

LEVEL	**Intermediate and above**
TIME	**40–50 minutes**
SKILLS	**Speaking**
OUTLINE	The teacher reads a letter aloud to the students while they are engaged in another task. They then make up a story based on words or phrases they remember, or associate with the text.
PREPARATION	Find a reasonably long letter, or part of a letter, with a strong narrative element. If your class is intermediate or above, you could use our example text below. Make an overhead projector transparency of it, or one copy for every two students.

... One other early memory of you ... taking me to see great-great-grandmother. Everybody was sitting around an oval table, and talking with great-grandmother at the head. She handed me a plate of cakes, and seeing that they had currants, I said 'No thank-you'. She said she had made them, and I must. So I took one, and while everyone was talking I quietly set to, and picked all the currants out so I could eat the cake. Great grannie suddenly saw what I was doing, and leaned down the length of the table and hit my hands with her stick. I jumped up and ran out into the kitchen and there was someone there to whom I cried, kneeling with my head in her lap.

On the way back to Nanny, I was feeling so ruffled, that I tried to jump off the moving bus, to get you irritated. The bus stopped, you rescued me, and were cross naturally, and the whole bus load of people were murmuring and sympathising with me being with a young man who hadn't the faintest idea how to look after me.

I remember very vividly knowing how they all blamed you for what I had done ... And when we got back Nanny couldn't believe I had been so naughty and also thought that you must have messed up the whole afternoon.

Do you remember it? One of the other dreadful things about that afternoon, or was it another ... was that I had to kiss that poor scarred face of my grandfather's wife. I felt physically sick even as a very little girl. Nasty little wretch, wasn't I? ...

PROCEDURE

1 Ask the students to doodle on a theme connected with your text. (As our text is about childhood memories, we asked our students to doodle on the theme of 'childhood'.) Explain that as they doodle you are going to read a letter aloud. They need pay no conscious attention.

2 Read the letter or extract aloud but unobtrusively.

3 When you have finished reading, pause and ask the students to show their doodles to a partner and explain what they represent, if anything.

4 Ask them to list any words they remember or associate with the text you read. Get the students to share their words and to add any to their own lists that they particularly like.

5 Pair the students. Ask them to use words from other lists to tell a story. This story can be as similar to, or different from, the one you read out (and which they may have half-heard) as they wish.

6 Each pair tells their story to another pair (or to the whole group if it is small enough).

7 Display the text you read on an overhead projector, or hand out photocopies.

COMMENTS

We don't know why people pick up so much when told they don't need to listen, but the technique works. It seems to be particularly successful with people who hate classrooms.

Acknowledgements

We would like to thank Adriana Diaz for the idea of not listening while doodling.

2.12 Frozen scenes

LEVEL

Intermediate

TIME

50–60 minutes

SKILLS

All

OUTLINE

Half the class read a letter, then represent it in silent, frozen scenes. The other students write the letter they imagine lies behind the scenes while the group who enacted them reconstruct the original letter from memory.

PREPARATION

Find a letter, part of a letter, or postcard with a strong central theme, or use the example below which is on the theme of giving. Make copies for half the class.

> Dear Sam,
>
> I am sure that the enclosed will come as a surprise to you – Welcome, I hope. Herewith small explanation. I have left little legacies to Peter, Leonie, and you, and it has occurred to me how much more useful it would be to have a small advance now rather than wait until I die. This is pure selfishness as I can enjoy the giving and there will still be a little left later.
>
> So don't make a fuss and hurt my feelings will you. I thought it might help with the word processing difficulty.
>
> Still waiting for appointment from hospital. The doctor said about six more days so should not be long now.
>
> It was lovely talking to Cathy. I wish you were nearer, but have many kind friends all willing to do things for me if necessary.
>
> Lots of love to you and Cathy.
>
> Mary

PROCEDURE

1 As a warm-up, choose a pair of contrasting themes: for example 'friendship vs. jealousy'; 'energy vs. fatigue'; 'heat vs. cold'. Ask three students to come out and express the idea of one of the themes in a silent, frozen scene. All three of them should take part. They should choose positions that they can hold for 10 to 15 seconds. Then ask another three students to represent its opposite, also in tableau form.

2 Give half the students a copy of the letter. Ask them to go outside and work in threes to produce a tableau that they feel represents the central message of the letter. Ask the threesomes to all work independently. Tell them they have 15 minutes to read and understand the letter and to produce the tableaux. You stay in class and do 15 minutes' revision with the other half of the group.

3 Ask the students who have prepared the tableaux to come back into the classroom and present their work. Make sure each group holds its tableau for at least 15 seconds, so that the audience have time to take in what is being presented.

4 Ask the students who have not read the letter to imagine the events behind the tableaux they have seen. They work in pairs to write a letter describing these imagined events.

5 Meanwhile, collect in the copies of the original letter from the tableaux students and ask them to reconstruct it from memory, also working in pairs. Be available to help both groups of students with language.

6 Bring the imaginative writers and the reconstructors back together: working in small groups, they read each others' texts.

7 Read the original letter to the whole class. Ask them to stop you when there is anything they do not understand or would like to comment on.

2.13 Rhythms

LEVEL	**Intermediate and above**
TIME	**50–60 minutes**
SKILLS	**Speaking, listening, reading**
OUTLINE	Students practise sentence stress by fitting fragments of imaginary dialogue to various rhythms.
PREPARATION	Find a postcard, or part of a letter with narrative content. We used the postcard from Rajasthan overleaf.
PROCEDURE	1 Read the text out to the class, asking them to take notes on what they hear.

2 Ask the students to get into groups of four and to compare their notes. Then write up the text on the board, or use an overhead transparency, and get them to check what they heard.

3 Clap out a simple rhythm and repeat it several times. It may help to have a phrase or short sentence in mind to clap to, for example 'OFF we go!' or 'Give me a BREAK!'

4 Ask the students, in their groups, to recall an event in the text you read out and to imagine a short sentence that could have been spoken at the time. For example, remembering the camel ride in the postcard from Rajasthan they might invent the sentence 'I'm going to fall OFF', or, recalling the shooting stars, 'LOOK at those STARS!'

5 Check that their sentences are correct, particularly the stress patterns, then ask the students, one group at a time, to clap out the rhythm of their sentences. Get the rest of the class to guess the words they have in mind.

6 Put some of the sentences on the board and get the rest of the class to repeat them after you, paying particular attention to sentence stress.

> You can't see me because I've just gone off to have a drink — but I was there and have the saddle sores to prove it. For two and a half days Pepo the Camel and I were thrown together. The best bit was getting off. Ate around a camp fire, played cards in a flickering light, and went to sleep to the shooting stars.
>
> Love
> Hester

COMMENTS

During normal conversation we are constantly having to guess at words which we have not heard properly. To do this, we often use the technique of guessing from stress patterns. This activity encourages students to practise doing this.

2.14 Complaining or praising

LEVEL

All

TIME

30–60 minutes

SKILLS

All

OUTLINE

Students choose products from a catalogue and write formal and/or informal letters complaining about or praising them.

PREPARATION

Get hold of a mail-order catalogue which you can tear up. If you have a monolingual class, and do not have easy access to mail-order catalogues in English, use one in the students' first language. Make sure there is at least one page of advertisements for every two students.

PROCEDURE

1 Tell the students to work in pairs, and give each pair a page of mail-order advertisements. Tell them to imagine that they have bought two of the products advertised, one of which they are delighted with, while the other has been a disaster. Encourage them to use their imaginations.

2 Ask them to write one or more of the following letters:
– a letter of appreciation—the kind of letter which the company might use to advertise the product
– a formal letter of complaint to the company telling of the unfortunate consequences of the purchase
– an informal letter to a friend reporting on an excellent, or a disastrous, buy.

3 Ask the students to display their letters so that others can read them. You could ask the class to vote for the most imaginative letter.

COMMENTS

Examination tasks frequently require candidates to write letters of complaint. This activity provides good practice, but is also fun because it offers students the chance to 'go over the top' in praise or criticism. It worked particularly well with a teenage class, who enjoyed letting their imaginations run riot!

3 Letters across the classroom

The basic idea behind this chapter is that a writer needs a reader and that an available and natural reader is another member of the class. Teachers who believe in a communicative classroom are happy to see students talking to each other in pairs, and we have come to feel the same about students writing to each other across the classroom. We maintain that the same communicative principles that inform oral work should inform the written mode. Many writing courses have students writing without an addressee, which simply makes the task harder for most people.

You might object that it is absurd to have people who can communicate orally writing to each other across the room. The amazing thing is that, once the students have got used to the oddity of the situation, they really do express themselves differently, and often more fully, in writing than they would do orally. The shy individuals blossom, as do students who need time to compose their thoughts and language. Letter writing also gives the class a break from orally dominant individuals. But students need not be confined to writing to each other. There are ideas here for starting up correspondences with you, the teacher, and even writing to themselves—writing can be a form of inner dialogue as well as a means of communicating with other people.

If you are running a course that leads to a written exam, you may find the ideas in this chapter helpful as they allow you to establish a class culture of students writing to each other and being read by each other. The activities presented here are designed to get the students writing to each other as naturally as they talk to each other in the foreign language. This allows them to find a written voice in English, which can then be adapted to the particular types of writing they have to do for the exam.

The activities in this chapter are divided into two groups: those for use early in the course, and those for use at any time. There are many more ways of launching and sustaining a letter-writing culture than we have space to set out here: our main contribution is perhaps not the set of activities but the letter-writing state of mind. If your students acquire this, you will find that plenty of new activities will suggest themselves.

For use early in the course

3.1 A 'model' letter

LEVEL   **Elementary to intermediate**

TIME   **5–15 minutes in class plus homework**

SKILLS   **Writing from a model**

OUTLINE   You give the students a 'model' letter for them to edit so that it becomes true about each of them. This letter could start a correspondence between them and you.

PREPARATION   Either write a model letter of your own, or use Worksheet 3.1. Make enough copies for all the students.

PROCEDURE   1 Give out the copies of the model letter and ask the students to read it in class. Help them with comprehension difficulties.

2 For homework, ask them to rewrite the letter. Tell them to keep the parts that make sense in their case and to change all the rest. Their version of the letter should be a sensible one to you about themselves.

3 In the next class, take in all the letters and answer them. (See 3.2, 'Dear Everybody', for more ideas on this.)

COMMENTS   We have found that if you start a correspondence with students by simply asking them to write a letter to the teacher, some of them don't know what to say and end up saying not very much. Giving them a model to destroy and at the same time to draw on linguistically makes the first letter easier to write in an informative way.

3.2 Dear Everybody

LEVEL   **All**

TIME   **5 minutes in lesson 1 plus homework**
15–30 minutes in lesson 2

SKILLS   **Writing and reading**

OUTLINE	Your students write you letters to which you reply with a single letter to the whole group, quoting from some of their letters. (This works best as an ongoing activity.)
PREPARATION	**(Between lessons 1 and 2)** Read the students' letters and write a 'Dear Everybody' letter in reply. You need to budget 5–10 minutes' writing time per student letter quoted in your answer. Make enough copies of your reply for each student to have one.
PROCEDURE	**Lesson 1** 1 Ask the students to each write you a letter as homework. Explain that the content of the letter is entirely up to the individual, but that when you answer the letters, with a single reply to the whole class, you will be quoting from some of them. **Lesson 2** 2 Give out the copies of your response and let the students read silently. If you have a class of 20 or less, simply be available to give the students individual help with comprehension. In larger classes, you may want to pre-teach some of the harder bits of language. 3 Ask the students to answer your letter for homework. The correspondence can continue for as long as you, and they, decide.
VARIATION 1	Ask the students, for homework, to write you a letter. Answer each letter individually. This individual correspondence can then carry on at a mutually agreeable pace. For further information about this technique, see Seth Lindstromberg: *The Recipe Book* (1990), page 85.
VARIATION 2	Use the technique described in Variation 1 with selected students with whom you feel you get better contact via the written channel. If you are a teacher-trainer, you may find this idea useful with certain trainees.
VARIATION 3	Ask the whole group to write to one student. The student replies, quoting slices of other students' letters and commenting on them, or using them as springboards for further thought.
COMMENTS	1 The techniques outlined in the Procedure grew out of Variation 1. However, we have found that answering individual students' letters can be both time-consuming and emotionally draining. It is also a secret communication between the teacher and individuals in the class and this may detract from the life of the group.

2 A serious danger in the main activity above is that the teacher may quote things that the students may not really want quoted, or omit things they would like the rest of the class to know. You need to exercise care and tact in your reply to the class.

3 Students will regularly ask to have their work back corrected. In his testing of the technique, Mario has refused to do this on the following grounds. The aim of this activity is self-expression in English, with the students attempting to say what maybe they can't yet say with any degree of accuracy. In some students, correction can produce a desire to write for the red pencil and not for the real addressee (the teacher, and beyond the teacher, the other students). And if the teacher corrects the letter, it has to be returned to the writer, which is a pretty odd thing to do in communication terms. But if you *really* want to correct the letters, then work on photocopies and give those back.

Extract from a letter to first week students:

Dear Everybody,

How would you feel if you had just received 13 letters from people you are to think about a lot over 10 weeks? Some people leave ample margins down the sides of their letters, while others fill the whole space, left and right. Some people have strong, flowing handwriting, while others make their letters small and tight.

It was nice of you, Kaholi, to be so open and honest about your first impressions. I'll try hard not to be too strict and stubborn! Stubbornness is one of my characteristics, and in some situations it can be useful.

Today has been an important day for me. My wife, Sophie, had her fifty-first birthday party and our five-and-a-half year-old son was quite excited about it. What are birthdays without small kids around? I shopped and cooked veal in Marsala (a sweet wine) ...

Extract from the seventeenth teacher letter in the same correspondence:

```
Dear Everybody,

Welcome back, Miho. Your absence was beginning to
weigh on me. The group is different without
Simona, too, isn't it? It is very hard to define
exactly how the disappearance of one person
affects one, but that there is an effect is
undeniable.

Yes, Atsuko, Simona had proved that she wants to
reach out beyond her cosy little western European
sphere by deciding to study Russian. She is
clearly very much involved with the language and
with the literature.

Good letter from you, again, Kanako. I really
think you have now reached take-off point: you
are getting airborne in English. Do you feel the
way the language flows now? When friends you have
known for a long time fall away from you it is a
very sad time. Yes, I have had this experience
with people who were very dear to me at
university who I now never see ...
```

(This was an intermediate class and they did not find the letters easy reading, linguistically. Ego needs and interest in others drew them into intensive reading—often!)

3.3 Co-operative writing

LEVEL	**All**
TIME	**40 minutes in lesson 1** **30–40 minutes in subsequent lessons**
SKILLS	**All**
OUTLINE	Small groups of students write joint letters to the teacher.
PREPARATION	None.
PROCEDURE	**Lesson 1** 1 Get the students up and moving about. Tell them they are to form threesomes that will stay together over the course or term in order, from time to time, to write letters to you, the teacher.

2 Ask the threesomes to write their first letter to you. Give them a 30-minute time limit. Tell them they can write about anything that interests all three of them.

3 At the end of the lesson, take in the letters. If you have a class of 30, you will have 10 letters to respond to. Photocopy your responses so that each student gets their own copy.

Subsequently

4 The correspondence between you and the threesomes can continue, either as homework or classwork.

Acknowledgements

We learnt the idea of students sharing the letter-writing process from Herbert Puchta.

3.4 Forward to the past

LEVEL	**Intermediate and above**
TIME	**20–40 minutes**
SKILLS	**Writing and reading**
OUTLINE	Students at the start of a course write letters to each other *looking back* over the course, as if they were writing after it has ended.
PREPARATION	None.

PROCEDURE

1 Early on in a course, before friendships have formed, ask the students to talk about their expectations of the course in pairs. Student A talks while Student B listens and encourages. Student B then talks while Student A listens.

2 Ask each student to imagine that the course is over. Then tell them to write a letter to a friend made in the group in which they describe some of their experiences and feelings during the course. Correct the students' writing individually as they work.

3 Tell the students to leave their letters on their desks. Students then go round reading each others' letters.

4 Ask the students to keep their letters. At the end of the course, tell them to look at the letters again. It will probably boost their confidence to see how much their English has improved. They may also be interested to see whether or not their predictions were right!

COMMENTS

You may feel that looking backwards into the future is an odd thing to do. We have found that the change in time perspective allows students to explore their expectations. Another aspect of this activity is that people make explicit to themselves and others some of their friendly feelings towards other students.

3.5 What do you think of the show so far?

LEVEL

All

TIME

30–40 minutes in lesson 1
5 minutes in lesson 2

SKILLS

Writing and reading

OUTLINE

Students write letters to each other about the course, with a copy to you.

PREPARATION

None.

PROCEDURE

Lesson 1
1 Ask each student to write a letter about the course so far to a person of their choice in the group. Tell the students that their letters will be copied for you to read too.

2 The students deliver their letters and the recipients read them. You then take in the letters for copying.

Lesson 2
3 In the next class, return the letters to their addressees.

COMMENTS

By asking the students to write feedback thoughts to classmates, you are tapping into the warmth of their relationships with others in the group. By not yourself being the direct recipient of the feedback, you may considerably enrich it.

VARIATION 1

With teenagers, ask them to write a letter to a member of their family describing what they feel about the class. These are shared round the group before being sent to the person concerned, with a translation into the mother tongue if necessary.

VARIATION 2

The same as Variation 1, except that the students know from the outset that the letter will not go to the addressee.

3.6 Write now, read later!

LEVEL   **All**

TIME   **20–30 minutes in lesson 1**
10–15 minutes in lesson 2

SKILLS   **Mainly writing and reading**

OUTLINE   Early in the course or term, the students write a letter to themselves which they 'receive' later on.

PREPARATION   Have an envelope ready for each student.

PROCEDURE   **Lesson 1**
1 In a lesson near the start of a course or term, ask the students to write private letters to themselves which they will receive in the middle, or towards the end of the course or term. The content of the letter is entirely in their hands. Be available to give language help, but don't look over people's shoulders unless asked to.

2 Give out the envelopes so that the students can address them and seal their letters inside. Collect the letters, and keep them in a safe place.

Lesson 2 (towards the end of the course)
3 The students receive the letters they wrote to themselves near the start of the course. Remind them that these were written to be private, but make it clear that they are free to share what they wrote if they feel like doing so.

VARIATION 1   Each student picks the name of a classmate from a hat and writes a letter to him or her. Collect in the letters and, after a few days, give them to their addressees.

VARIATION 2   On the last day of a course in an English-speaking country, each student writes a letter to themselves back at home the following week, and the letter is posted to their home address.

VARIATION 3   Instead of using the technique outlined above as a one-off activity, get the students to do it regularly over a course or a term. They will end up with a diary of the passing weeks.

VARIATION 4   At the beginning of lesson 1 bring in a sealed envelope addressed to yourself, open it in class, and read out a letter you apparently wrote to yourself two months ago.

This is a dramatic and very clear way of getting over the idea of writing a letter to oneself to receive at a later date.

COMMENTS	To read a letter you wrote yourself last week, or six weeks ago, can have a real time-travel effect. It is not just what you wrote, it is the way the letter takes you back to the situation you were in then, to the feeling and atmosphere of that time.

3.7 Letters about letters

LEVEL	**Intermediate and above**
TIME	**5 minutes in lesson 1, plus homework** **15 minutes in lesson 2**
SKILLS	**Reading and writing**
OUTLINE	Students answer a letter from the teacher about their own letter-writing habits.
PREPARATION	Make a copy of Worksheet 3.7 for each of your students.
PROCEDURE	**Lesson 1** 1 Give each student a copy of Worksheet 3.7 and ask them to reply to the letter individually for homework. **Lesson 2** 2 Group the students in fours or fives to read each others' letters about letters. You may decide to use these student letters as a starting-off point for a correspondence with them.

3.8 Imagine we've met before

LEVEL	**Intermediate and above**
TIME	**40–50 minutes**
SKILLS	**All, but especially writing**
OUTLINE	Students pick a person to write to and describe a fantasy previous meeting.
PREPARATION	None.
PROCEDURE	1 Put this picture on the board.

Elicit all possible ways of saying 'Hello, remember me?', and drill it.

2 As a warm-up activity, pair the students at random and ask them to imagine they have met before but can't immediately 'remember' where or when. They 'remind' each other. After a few minutes, ask them to change partners and repeat the activity. Get them to change partners frequently until they have relaxed and become inventive.

3 Ask the students to write a letter to someone else in the class. In the letter, they should describe a fantasized previous meeting with him or her. Allow between 20 and 30 minutes.

4 Tell the students to either deliver their letters by hand, or hand them in for marking as they wish. If the students agree, you could display their letters for the rest of the class to read.

3.9 Getting to know you better

LEVEL	**Intermediate and above**
TIME	**60 minutes**
SKILLS	**All**
OUTLINE	Students interview a classmate, then write a letter describing them.
PREPARATION	None.
PROCEDURE	1 Ask the students to pair up with a person they know well, or who they would like to get to know better. Explain that they are going to write a letter about that person. The letter could be to you, or to someone else the whole class knows, for example another teacher. Give them 10 minutes to interview each other, either finding out new facts, or checking those they already know.

2 Give the students 15–20 minutes to organize their notes into a plan, deciding which pieces of information should go into which paragraphs of their letter.

3 Explain that they have 15 minutes to write the letter from their plans. As in an examination, they must work on their own in silence. Tell them they may use a dictionary.

4 Ask the students to reread their letters and to underline a maximum of three phrases that they think need correction. Tell them, for each phrase, to try to think of an alternative way of saying the same thing. They should then decide which of the alternatives is preferable in terms of comprehensibility and correctness. As they do this, walk around giving help where it is needed.

5 Get the students to swap work, read the letter about themselves, and write a comment on the bottom if they want to.

6 Ask the students to leave the letters about themselves on their desks and walk around reading the other letters. Tell them to jot down expressions they particularly like or are impressed by.

7 To round off the activity, have a brief feedback discussion with the whole class.

COMMENTS

In our experience, students are very good at spotting weaknesses in their own written work. The aim of step 4 is to train them to have a little more confidence in their ability to check, correct, or reformulate their own work. This is a useful skill for examinations.

For use at any time

3.10 Battle of the sexes

LEVEL

Intermediate and above

TIME

40–50 minutes

SKILLS

All

OUTLINE

Students discuss a questionnaire before writing a letter to someone of the opposite sex about being the sex they are.

PREPARATION

Make one copy of Worksheet 3.10 for each pair of students.

PROCEDURE

1 Divide the class into male and female groups. Ask the students to get into pairs within their groups, and give out one copy of the questionnaire to each pair. The students work through it.

2 Ask each student to write a letter to a member of the opposite sex on what they feel about being the sex they are.

3 Organize the students in mixed-sex groups of six to eight people. Each person reads out the letter they have written. This may lead to general discussion.

COMMENTS

1 In this activity, letter-writing serves as a quiet, slow, reflective phase, sandwiched between the initial same-sex work on the letter or questionnaire, and the final mixed discussion.

2 You need to know your students well before using this activity.

3.11 Changing sex

LEVEL

Intermediate and above

TIME

40–50 minutes

SKILLS

All

OUTLINE

Each person is interviewed in the role of a person of the opposite sex who they know well. They then write a letter to the person they have been role-playing.

PREPARATION

None.

PROCEDURE

1 Get the students up and moving about. Ask them each to find a partner they feel comfortable with. (Moving round the room allows students to choose a partner freely—they don't feel obliged to choose their neighbour.)

2 Explain that person A in each pair is to choose a person of the opposite sex to role-play. This should be a person they know well, but not another member of the class. They should sit like the person they have chosen to role-play and try to talk the way that person would. Get two or three students to show how their person would sit and to describe what he or she might be wearing.

3 Student B in each pair now interviews student A's role-character. The content of the interview is totally open, but can cover areas such as present situation, background, childhood, and relationships with people of the opposite sex. The interview should last 10 to 15 minutes.

4 They then change over so that student A interviews and student B role-plays.

5 Ask the students to write a letter to the person they have just role-played. Tell them this letter will be entirely private—neither you, nor anyone else in the group will see it. If they want your help with language, they can simply write the sentence they want help with on a separate sheet of paper. In this way you can be technically useful without invading their privacy.

COMMENTS

1 We feel that there should be times set aside in the language class when students write privately. Writing for yourself in the target language suggests you are really willing to make it your own.

2 As with 3.10 'Battle of the sexes', you need to know your students well before using this activity in class. Students from some cultures may find the concept of 'changing sexes' difficult, even offensive.

3.12 To me at three

LEVEL

Intermediate and above

TIME

45–90 minutes

SKILLS

All

OUTLINE

Students talk about early memories and then write to themselves at that age from the present.

PREPARATION

None.

PROCEDURE

1 Tell the class one of your earliest memories. Give them time to absorb it and to ask for clarification if necessary.

2 Ask the students to find a partner and take it in turns to spend precisely three minutes each talking uninterruptedly about their earliest memory. The listener should give full attention to his or her partner and remain silent if the speaker needs time to pause and reflect.

3 Ask the students to change partners and do the activity again. They can either tell the same story again or, if an earlier memory presents itself, change to that.

4 Ask the students to change partners again and to do the activity a third time, but this time they should refer to themselves in the third person, for example instead of 'I was taken to ...', 'He/she was taken to ...' . Remind them they are free to change to another memory whenever an earlier one presents itself.

5 Invite the students to recount their earliest memory to the whole group, but do not try and force anyone who is reluctant to do this.

6 Ask the students to write a letter to themselves at the age of their earliest memory. They should write from where they are now, knowing what they now know.

7 Invite the students to display their letter on their desk or the wall so that others can read it, or to exchange letters with a partner they have not worked with during this lesson.

8 Ask whether anybody remembers more of their early life now than they did at the beginning of the lesson.

9 If anyone looks as if they are finding it hard to come out of their memories, finish off the session by pulling their attention into the present. Here are some suggestions for how to do this:

- Ask them to tell the class about their favourite TV programme/recipe/outfit and to work out exactly when they last watched/cooked/wore it.
- Ask them to list all the objects they can see and name in one minute.

VARIATION

You may like to leave the writing exercise for homework. If you do this, remember not to leave out step 8 (and 9 if necessary) as it is important to bring the students back into the present.

COMMENTS

1 This is an adaptation of a co-counselling exercise.

2 We have found that some students cannot remember being very young at first, but gradually their memories get earlier. If someone protests that they have no really early memories, then encourage them to tell the earliest they have available, or allow them to spend the time explaining that they are unable to bring any to mind. It may help to give them the line 'I have no memories at all before the age of ...'

3 It is important that the students do not perceive this activity as a competition for the earliest or for the most entertaining anecdote. The emphasis should be on empathetic listening skills rather than on the accuracy of the language used in the telling. The role of the teacher is to model good listening, to take or delegate responsibility for timing (which should be tight), and above all to participate.

3.13 At a different age

LEVEL

Elementary and above

TIME

40–60 minutes in lesson 1
10–20 minutes in lesson 2

SKILLS

Writing and reading

OUTLINE

Students choose an age they would like to be. They write letters to others in the class from the age of their choice and are written to at the same age.

PREPARATION

None.

PROCEDURE

Lesson 1

1 If you have a large class, divide the students into sub-groups of 10 to 15. If possible, get each group to sit in a circle so that they can see each others' faces.

2 Ask each student to decide on an age they feel like being (older, or younger, than their real age). Explain that they will be writing letters to other people in their sub-group from the standpoint of that age. Also explain that they should address other students at the ages *they* have chosen. Ask everyone to write a label with their name and chosen age in large letters and either pin it to themselves or put it on the desk in front of them.

3 Students write letters to each other within their sub-groups. Make yourself available to help with language. In our experience, students need a lot of help with register. As soon as a student has finished a letter they should deliver it. The receiver may well want to reply. At the end of the lesson, collect the letters.

Lesson 2

4 Use two or three of the letters written in the previous lesson to teach the students more about appropriate written register.

VARIATION 1

Ask the students to write letters to each other in role as another member of their family who is of the opposite sex. So, for example, a Spanish student, Juan, might choose the role of his aunt, Maria Jesús. As in the activity above, the students write labels for themselves in role. So Juan would write 'Doña Maria Jesús, Juan's aunt'.

VARIATION 2

Tell the students that today, for half an hour, they can be another person and write in role as that person. They can change such things as their social class, historical period, sex, age, or religion. Again, they write labels for themselves so other students are clear about who they are writing to.

VARIATION 3

Put pictures of well-known figures, from past or present, round the walls. Students choose a figure they feel like impersonating and go and sit below it. In role, they then write a letter to another figure that has a student sitting below it. Correspondences ensue.

VARIATION 4

Students who are studying a novel or a play write to each other as one of the characters. What might a student Portia write to a student Shylock?

Acknowledgements

Variation 2 is based on an oral exercise we learnt from Elayne Phillips, who trained two of us. Variation 3 comes from student work directed by Sue Leather.

3.14 From a leaf to a tree

LEVEL

Intermediate and above

TIME

50–60 minutes

SKILLS

All

OUTLINE

Students write letters to each other in class in role as a leaf or a tree.

PREPARATION

Collect twigs or branches from common trees to take into class.

PROCEDURE

1 Ask some students to come to the board and draw their favourite trees and name them in English. Check they can name the parts of the tree, for example: roots, trunk, branch, bud, bark.

2 Pass the twigs and branches you have brought in round the group. Ask the students to identify which trees they come from.

3 Get everybody up and moving around the room. Tell them to each find a partner. One person in each pair is to role-play being a tree and the other the leaf or needle of the same tree.

The partners go back to their normal places and write each other letters in role, tree to leaf and leaf to tree.

4 As the students finish writing their letters, each tree exchanges letters with their leaf. They answer each other's letters.

5 When the answers have been written, ask the students to stick the groups of four letters up round the walls and to read and enjoy as many of the correspondences as they can.

VARIATION 1

Instead of pairing the students at the start of the activity, divide the class into two halves: one half are the trees and the other half are the leaves. The leaves write letters to the trees and the trees write letters to the leaves. As soon as a student has finished, they should give their letter to a student in the other group who has also just finished. The partners then reply to each other's letters.

VARIATION 2

Allow the students to choose whether they want to write as a leaf or as a tree. When they have written their first letter, they reply to their own letter in role as the receiver of the first letter, so if they first wrote as a tree they reply as a leaf.

VARIATION 3

Parts of any whole can write to the whole, or to other parts. The chassis of a car might write to the car, or to the steering wheel, the clutch, or the brakes. If the river were the whole, a meander might write to it, or to a waterfall, an estuary, or rapids.

COMMENTS

Students are usually asked to do things in English that they have done many times in their own language. There is no sense of new self-expression. This activity is something they have probably never done before in any language, and consequently English is being used to explore.

Dear Fir tree!

I'm one of your needles. I've understood the situation. I'm packing up. I'm going to leave you in a few days. Direction North! Another fir tree, a relative of mine, is waiting for me to celebrate together the Christmas time. With this write I want to say you goodbye and to thank you for all you've done for me.

See you,
Yours, Needle

> Dear Leaf
>
> It looks like the men are coming to get me, because I saw them when they finished their day's work yesterday and they were just three rows from me, so I think that today they are going to beat me to make my olives fall down. I am writing to you because you can fall down with the olives and will die because you will not be able to eat anymore from my branches. I want to tell you that it has been very nice for me having you in my branches and being part of me. Don't be afraid — maybe you can survive the fight that I have to suffer every year at this time.
> Good luck, yours,
>
> Tree.

3.15 Different walks

LEVEL	**All**
TIME	**40–50 minutes**
SKILLS	**All**
OUTLINE	Students introduce three people to their partner by imitating their walks. The partner chooses one of the three, and is written to as from that person.
PREPARATION	None.
PROCEDURE	1　Take the students to a space where they can walk freely, out of doors perhaps.

2　Ask one student to stand close behind you and to imitate the walk you are going to do. He or she should walk as close behind you as possible.

3 Now imagine you are going to walk with a person you know well. You feel good to be with them and you walk exactly as they are walking. Start walking like this person, with a feeling of their presence beside you and the look of their face in your mind's eye. The student behind you imitates the walk.

4 Explain to the students that they are to work in pairs. One student imagines themselves walking with three people they know well, and copies, in turn, each one's way of walking. The other student imitates the walks, staying as close behind as possible. The pair must walk long enough for the student behind to really feel each style of walking. The student in front does not tell their partner anything about the three people he or she is thinking of.

5 The students then swap roles.

6 Once the pairs have done their six walks, ask each student to choose the walk they imitated which most intrigued them.

7 Take the students back to the classroom and tell them that, as owner of the walk their partner has chosen, they are going to write a letter in role as the person they were thinking of. They should introduce themselves in their letters.

8 The students then give their letters to their partners and the pairs talk about the person presented through the chosen walk. If there is time, they can talk about the people who were not chosen as well.

COMMENTS

There may be some of your students for whom walking in the English lesson may be a relief. Writing will come as a relief to those students who don't initially see much point in waddling around aping other people's way of walking. The talking phase will feel good to those who find the written medium too slow and painstaking. The three main activities balance each other and form a neat lesson whole.

Acknowledgements

We learnt the germ of this exercise from Mike Shreeve on an NLP course at Pilgrim's. He called it 'In your moccasins' and used it to help us mirror other people and to get on their wavelength.

3.16 Maths letters

LEVEL

Intermediate and above

TIME

40–50 minutes

SKILLS

All

OUTLINE

Students write to each other about how they feel as Maths learners.

PREPARATION

None.

PROCEDURE

1 Pair the students. Show them your hand and ask them to work out how many combinations of three fingers they can find in the five fingers of one hand: for example one combination is thumb, forefinger, and middle finger. Give no help with how to solve the problem. (Students usually come up with answers between 8 and 20. The correct answer is 10.)

2 Ask the students to recall the people who have taught them Maths. Ask how many Maths teachers they have each had. Ask four or five people to describe the Maths teachers they remember most clearly.

3 Tell the students who feel good about Maths to sit on one side of the room and the students who don't to sit on the other. Ask them to write letters to students in the other group about how they feel as Maths learners.

4 Round off the lesson by getting the students to put up their exchanges of letters on the wall so that the whole class can share them.

VARIATION

Instead of Maths, take other areas which some people find difficult and others find comparatively easy, for example learning to drive—or learning a language!

Acknowledgements

We learnt the finger combination exercise from Dick Tachta, a Silent Way Maths teacher.

3.17 Unfinished letters

LEVEL

Intermediate and above

TIME

40–60 minutes

SKILLS

Writing and reading

OUTLINE

Each student receives a letter addressed to them by another student, but only half-written. They finish it in the same mind-set and style.

PREPARATION

None.

PROCEDURE

1 Ask the students to find a partner they are happy to work with for the rest of the lesson.

2 Ask them to sit apart from their partner and start a letter to them. Tell them they have at least 30 minutes to write this letter.

3 After 15 minutes, ask the students to stop writing and to exchange their letters with their partners. The partner now continues writing the letter to themselves as if they were the other person. Tell them to maintain the same style, and to try to feel and understand how the original writer would want the letter to continue to its conclusion.

4 The partners now come together and compare what they have done. They also check over each other's writing for mistakes.

5 Each pair joins up with another pair and they see what the other two have done.

3.18 To myself as if from someone else

LEVEL

All

TIME

30–40 minutes

SKILLS

All

OUTLINE

Each student takes on the role of another student in the class and writes to themselves from that role.

PREPARATION

Make sure there is a hat, a small bag, or something similar, for each group of eight to ten students.

PROCEDURE

1 Divide the students into groups of eight to ten. Tell them each to write their name on a small piece of paper, fold it, and put it in the hat.

2 Each student takes a name from the hat and assumes the role of that person.

3 In their assumed role, they write a letter to their real selves on any topic.

4 Students now give their letter to the person whose role they assumed. This person reads it out to the rest of the class or group.

5 Leave time for discussion at the end. Students often want to describe things which emerge from this activity, such as how they felt in another person's skin, and how they felt seeing themselves through another's eyes.

3.19 In three roles

LEVEL

All

TIME

50–60 minutes

SKILLS

Mainly reading and writing

OUTLINE

Students write to each other in three roles: as parent, child, and other parent.

PREPARATION

None.

PROCEDURE

1 Divide the class into groups of eight to ten, and get each group to sit in a circle.

2 Tell the students to imagine that the person on their left is their child. In role as either mother or father, they write a short letter to their 'child'.

3 When the 'parents' have finished their letters, they hand them to their left, to their 'children'. Everybody now assumes the role of child and writes an answer to their 'parent'.

4 When the 'children' have finished their letters, they hand them to their right, to their 'parents'.

5 Everybody now assumes the role of the parent of the opposite sex. For example, if they first wrote as 'mother', they now write as 'father'. They reply to their 'child's' letter, which was written to the other parent.

6 Everybody hands their letter to their left, to their 'child'.

7 Get the students to display their letters, so the rest of the class can read them.

VARIATION

You can do this activity with any three interlinked roles, for example a manager writes to his client about her decision not to place an order; the client replies; the Managing Director replies to the client.

COMMENTS

The beauty of this activity is that the students experience three different roles in quick succession, which allows them to write in three different voices.

1 Tomoko, in role as 'mother', writes to her 'son':

Dear K,

How is your life in England? Are you enjoying yourself? I hope so because you told us you wanted to go. How is your English? Is it improving?

Your grandmother, M, worries about you all the time. Have you written to her or telephoned?

I have sent you the parcel which you asked us for. It takes one month to get there. I wasn't able to find your leather boots in your closet. If you want to have them, why don't you buy new ones?

We are really fine, as usual. There is no problem. Recently your grandmother is going to a fitness gym for her health. She enjoys a lot and keeps fit. Your father is keen on playing golf and I like drinking a cup of tea which you sent us before.

Well, have fun and study hard.

Take care,

Lots of love.

Your mother, T.

2 Tomoko, in role as 'son', writes to her 'mother':

Dear Mum,

Thanks for your letter. I really relax when I read your letter.

Of course I am a little bit nervous about my exam. You know there are still parts of FCE exam. I hate it but our teacher is really nice. I enjoy every moment.

I also worry about my future when I go back. You told me that you were able to ask my cousin who works in the travel agency about my job. I am interested in working there but prefer there should be no relation between company and me. It is much better for me. I have written about my study in a university. Do you think it is a good idea to study at university? We have to talk about move, anyway.

I am really happy to live here. I have to say to you, or my father or grandfather, 'thank you'.

I hope that you are always happy and fine.

Merry Christmas and a Happy New Year. I know that the end of the year you are always busy. Take care and don't do housework too much.

See you in March.

Lots of love, T.

3 Tomoko, in role as 'father', writes to her 'son':

Dear K,

Your mum read your letter to me. Your English is actually getting better, I suppose.

How are you going to stay during your Christmas holiday? Have you booked flights to come back to Thailand? Or do you prefer to stay in England without anything to do?

You don't write to us so we don't usually know what you are doing. Write you a letter once every two weeks at least. When your uncle asked us about you, we weren't able to say anything. I just told him 'I hope he is fine because we haven't received his letter for one month'.

Take care, because you are in England not in Thailand.

Your father, T.

3.20 Some more ideas ...

Students write to each other freely in class

PROCEDURE

Give the students half a dozen small sheets of paper each. Tell them they have 20 to 30 minutes to write to any of their classmates in English. Once a letter has been written, it is signed and delivered. Students who receive letters often want to reply to them. Your classroom hums with fast, lively writing and reading.

VARIATION 1

In some groups, popular students get all the letters and others get very few. To reduce this tendency, start the activity by asking the students to all write a letter starting 'Dear Somebody', which they sign. Put all these letters in a pile. Each student takes one and answers it. They are then free to write to anybody in the group.

VARIATION 2

You can use the 'writing to each other' technique to launch a theme. You ask each student to write to one other person about the theme. Students who are happy to read out the letters they have received then do so.

Acknowledgements

These ideas are from Lindstromberg (ed.): *The Recipe Book* (Pilgrims-Longman 1990).

Ghost writing

PROCEDURE

1 Pair the students. Student A decides on a person in the group she wants to send a letter to. She tells Student B, her partner, to write to this person on her behalf. Student B writes as A, in the first person. Student A defines the content and tone of the letter.

2 Student B chooses a person in the group she wants Student A to write to on her behalf and tells A what to write.

3 They then *simultaneously* start penning letters as their partner's ghost writer.

4 When both have finished writing, they give the letters to each other for correction and signing. The letter originator may decide to correct and change things before signing. The letters are delivered.

5 People receiving letters reply via their ghost writer. It is vital that the students should be engaged in simultaneous writing; they should not end up dictating text to each other.

COMMENTS

This activity is particularly rich at upper-intermediate and advanced levels.

Acknowledgements

For a more detailed presentation of this idea, see Lindstromberg (ed.): *The Recipe Book* (Pilgrims-Longman 1990).

4 Letters out from the class

This chapter offers you a number of new ways of getting students to write to people beyond the walls of their classroom. Using an international language internationally makes clear and obvious sense: many secondary school teachers have recognized this in setting up pen-pal relationships for their classes. In this kind of letter-writing it is natural for students to really want to get their texts as correct as possible. The teacher suddenly becomes a supportive corrector rather than a partly wanted, judgemental one. In contrast to Chapter 3 'Letters across the classroom', where the emphasis is on helping the students to try and say things they can't yet easily say, the activities in this chapter foster a desire for accuracy and correctness.

Native speakers of English are the most obvious people to write to outside the classroom. If you are able to set up correspondences with several native speakers, then your students will receive genuine communications from a variety of people, each of whom writes in a characterisic way. The letters come in response to the things they have said and asked, and so are much more personal than coursebook texts. These correspondences can easily be given a cultural slant, with your students using the native speakers as sources for information on the life and institutions of their country.

However, native speakers are not the only correspondents we suggest in this chapter. Students studying in English-speaking environments usually write plenty of letters home in the mother tongue and also, of course, receive letters from home. Both these types of letter—or parts of them—can be translated and shared with the rest of the class. We have found that this kind of activity is only feasible in groups with plenty of trust, but when it does work, it produces an extraordinary reading climate. For example, Italian students are amazed to find that when Thai or Japanese mothers write to their daughters the voices are not that different from Italian ones. The exchange of translated letters in the writing class is one of the most moving cultural understanding activities we have witnessed.

Students go sick and are absent from class for long periods, they leave the school, they move abroad, or, if they are studying English abroad, they return home. Each time a student leaves the class, this creates a letter-writing opportunity for the rest. And eventually, of course, groups come to an end. Saying goodbye is not always easy, and doing so in writing is a way for both teachers and students to ease themselves out of the group situation, to think back over the work done together, and maybe say things they would not have been able to say face to face. If strong bonds have been forged during a course, teacher and students need ways to gain distance and perspective when the time comes to part company. The group of activities at the end of this chapter are specifically designed for use at the end of a course.

If you have access to the Internet, e-mail will really come into its own in many of the activities in this chapter. The whole correspondence process is speeded up enormously, and e-mail will appeal to those technologically-minded students who might find traditional letter-writing old-fashioned. See the Appendix on page 95.

For use at any time

4.1 Students write to a native speaker

LEVEL	**Intermediate and above**
TIME	**30–40 minutes in lesson 1** **15–20 minutes in lesson 2**
SKILLS	**All**
OUTLINE	The students write to a native speaker of English you know and receive a reply.
PREPARATION	Choose an English-speaking friend or relative. Make sure that they would enjoy receiving a batch of letters from your class, and would be willing to send a reply.
PROCEDURE	**Lesson 1** **1** Ask a student who is good at drawing to produce a picture of your relative or friend on the board, following your instructions. Describe what the person is like, what they do, and their relationship to you. **2** Tell the students they are going to write a letter to this person and that the letters will be sent. Make it clear that this is not a role-play activity. If necessary, help them with the appropriate formulas for starting and finishing their letters. For example, they will want to address a grandmother differently from a teenager.

3 While the students are writing, make yourself available for help and correction. In this activity, students tend to want plenty of both.

4 When the students have finished their letters, ask them if they are happy for their classmates to read what they have written. If they are, get them to leave their letters on their desks. They can move round, reading each others' letters. Collect and send the letters.

Lesson 2
5 When your friend or relative replies, photocopy their letter and let each student have a copy. Allow time for reading and comments. Alternatively, you could read the letter out to them.

VARIATION

Mario got his class to write to a nephew and the nephew's girlfriend. Some students wrote to him, some to her, and some to both.

Acknowledgements
This idea came from John Barnett.

4.2 Political letters

LEVEL

Intermediate and above

TIME

5 minutes in lesson 1 plus homework
40–50 minutes in lesson 2

SKILLS

Writing, reading, and motivated rewriting

OUTLINE

At a time of political watershed, students write letters to the leading people involved.

PREPARATION

None.

PROCEDURE

Lesson 1
1 On a day when your students will probably have seen a lot of TV and newspaper coverage of a major political change, ask them, for homework, to write short letters to one or more of the politicians involved. Examples might include a farewell letter to an outgoing leader and a letter of welcome to an incoming one. Tell them that the letters will actually be sent to the addressees.

Lesson 2
2 Group the students in sixes to read each other's letters and to react to their contents. Get the students correcting each other's mistakes and go round helping where you are needed.

3 Tell the students to produce fair copies of their letters.

4 Give the students envelopes so that they can send their letters.

5 If any of the students receive a reply, invite them to share it with the rest of the class.

<table>
<tr><td>VARIATION</td><td>Ask the students to write letters to people involved in major events in the world of sport.</td></tr>
</table>

VARIATION

Ask the students to write letters to people involved in major events in the world of sport.

Acknowledgements

We learnt this technique from Gerry Kenny who used it at the time of the inauguration of President Clinton and the retirement of President Bush. Gerry writes: 'The discussion that surrounded the writing and reading was astonishingly rich. The beauty of the activity came from the moment of the changeover, the feeling that really new things were in the offing.'

4.3 Letters to an author

LEVEL

Intermediate and above

TIME

5 minutes in lesson 1 plus homework
40–50 minutes in lesson 2
15–30 minutes in lesson 3

SKILLS

Mainly reading and writing

OUTLINE

Students read a poem, story, or diary extract and write a letter to the author giving their reactions.

PREPARATION

1 Choose an English-speaking writer who might like to receive letters from your students. You could choose a published author and contact them through their publisher, but you stand a better chance of receiving a reply if you choose an unknown poet, story-writer, or diarist who writes in English. It might be interesting, for example, to ask a teenage writer, or perhaps an older person who is willing to share their diary from many years ago.

2 Copy a text by the chosen author for the group. Prepare a covering letter to the author explaining that your students have read a text of theirs and written them a letter. Suggest that the students would love to receive a reply!

PROCEDURE

Lesson 1
1 Give out the text and ask the students to read it for homework. You could use more than one short text.

Lesson 2

2 Give the students some personal background about the author and ask them to react to the text or texts by writing the author a letter. Make it clear that you will send the letters to the writer, unless, having written theirs, an individual student decides it should not be sent. Be available to help with language problems. Collect the letters and send them off with your covering letter.

Lesson 3

3 If you receive an answer from the author, ask the students to reread the original text. Give them copies of the author's letter and help with any comprehension problems.

VARIATION 1

Use the material presented and generated in this activity with another group of students. First give the students the author's answer and ask them to guess what sort of text it refers to. Then give them some of the first group's letters and ask them the same question. Finally give them the text itself to read.

VARIATION 2

Ask the students to write to the author of their English coursebook.

COMMENTS

This activity works because an author is an obvious person to talk to about their writing and because many authors are thirsty for reader response, especially if they are unpublished.

Examples

The two letters below were written by lower-intermediate students, one Swiss and one Japanese, in response to a one-page, surrealistic story about a boss.

Dear Gerry,

I am a Swiss girl studying English in M's class at the Cambridge Academy. Today, in class, I read one of your stories, 'You are the boss, boss'. I think this is a funny story, but a bit strange. I couldn't understand a lot of it, not because of the language but because of the meaning. I have the feeling that the story could be continued, continued, continued… I have the feeling of a really stupid boss. Was that the idea of Boss you wanted to give us with this story? Anyway, I enjoyed it because I like strange things.

Do you often write such strange stories? Is this your hobby? I am looking forward to hear from you. See you.
A.

Gerry Kenny's answer to the students starts:

```
Dear Friends,

There can be very few unpublished authors who can
boast or even dream of receiving the quantities
of fan mail I recently received from all of you.
Thank you very, very much.

It is not easy to answer all of the questions you
ask in your letters, nor do I believe it to be
appropriate. People say that a single question
can generate a multitude of answers, but the same
question can also generate many further
questions. This is a story for people who like
asking questions ...
```

4.4 You don't know me but ...

LEVEL

Elementary and above (This activity is best for one-to-one teaching situations or for very small groups.)

TIME

5 minutes in lesson 1
30 minutes in lesson 2
15 minutes in lesson 3

SKILLS

All, and translation

OUTLINE

The student translates into English a letter they have recently received from someone they know well. The teacher writes in English to this person in consultation with the student, who then translates the teacher's letter into the language of the original letter.

PREPARATION

None.

PROCEDURE

Lesson 1
1 Ask the student to translate into English all or part of a personal letter they have recently received. Make it clear that they need not translate anything that they are unwilling to share with you.

Lesson 2
2 Go through the content of the translated letter with your student, encouraging explanation of the background and getting an idea of the writer.

3 Tell your student that you are now going to write to the person whose letter they have translated for you. You will send the letter only if your student wants it sent. Start writing straight away: 'Dear X, You don't know me, but ...'. Involve the student as much as you can in the writing.

4 Ask the student to edit your letter for homework and to translate it into the language spoken by the writer of the original letter.

Lesson 3

5 Ask the student where they had difficulties in translating your letter and help them sort these out. Send the letter, but only if the student is happy for you to do so.

VARIATION	**1** Ask the student to imagine that their parents or employer have written to you asking for an evaluation of their work on the course.
	2 Tell your student you will write your report as a letter, but that they must tell you what they want you to say in it. Make it clear to the student that this letter will not be sent. Keep checking with the student that what you have written really expresses their ideas, but make sure that you use your own words and style.
	3 Keep the letter for a week and then ask the student to translate it for homework. Setting the letter aside allows the student to return to it and re-evaluate what they think about their progress.

4.5 Home

LEVEL	**Elementary and above (For use with classes in English-speaking countries.)**
TIME	**5 minutes in lessons 1 to 4, plus homework after lessons 1 and 3** **30–45 minutes in lesson 5**
SKILLS	**All, and translation**
OUTLINE	Students translate parts of letters they have written home or which people at home have written to them. The class read the translations.
PREPARATION	None.

PROCEDURE

Lesson 1
1 For homework, ask the students to translate parts of letters they have written to people at home or which people at home have written to them. Explain that they should only choose content they are happy to share with the rest of the class.

Lesson 2
2 Take in the translated texts and correct them before the next class.

Lesson 3
3 Return the corrected texts to their writers and ask them, for homework, to copy out correct versions.

Lesson 4
4 Collect in the fair copies. Photocopy them for the group.

Lesson 5
5 Give the copies to their owners to share with the rest of the group. The students read the texts and ask the translators about any language or cultural problems.

COMMENTS

We have found that students read the translated texts with great care. We have also found that the translators are keen to incorporate the corrections into their fair copies. Who wants their grandfather speaking bad English to the group? The activity works best when there is an atmosphere of mutual trust in the group.

4.6 Translating postcards

LEVEL

Elementary to intermediate (For use with classes in English-speaking countries.)

TIME

5 minutes in lesson 1 plus homework
20–40 minutes in lesson 2

SKILLS

All, and translation

OUTLINE

Students write postcards in their own language to people back home. They produce both literal translations of the texts and idiomatic ones.

PREPARATION

None.

PROCEDURE

Lesson 1

1 Ask the students to think of four people at home they have not contacted since coming abroad, but who they would like to contact. Then ask them, for homework, to choose a postcard for each of these people and to write full messages to them in their mother tongue. Tell them that after the next lesson the cards can be sent to their addressees. Ask the students to bring the cards, and bilingual dictionaries, to the next lesson.

Lesson 2

2 Ask the students to choose the most interesting message of the four and to make a literal translation of it into English, keeping the word order of the mother-tongue version. They should choose a text they do not mind sharing with the rest of the class.

3 Ask them to make an idiomatic translation of the same text as well. Be available to help them produce authentic 'postcard English'.

4 Ask the students, in turn, to read out both their literal and their idiomatic translations. They pick out instances of where the two differ greatly, or where they are very similar. They also pick out expressions in English that they like. Ask the students to tell the group a bit about the people they have written to.

5 The original postcards are posted.

COMMENTS

This is a powerful language-awareness activity for a low-level international class. In particular, it helps the speakers of Indo-European languages to realize the contrastive difficulties faced by speakers of other language groups when learning English.

4.7 Unsent letters

LEVEL

Intermediate and above

TIME

30–50 minutes

SKILLS

Reading and writing

OUTLINE

Students write to people they would not normally write to, or letters they would enjoy writing but would probably not actually send.

PREPARATION

None.

PROCEDURE

1 Tell the students that they are going to write to someone that they would never send a letter to. Give them some of the ideas below, and invite them to add their own suggestions.

Write a letter:

– to someone who bugs you
– to someone you have hurt or offended
– to an ex-boyfriend, ex-girlfriend, or ex-friend
– to an unborn child
– to an examiner
– to a burglar who has 'done' your house
– to a person who helped you without knowing it
– to the present owner of the house you used to live in
– to a famous historical figure.

2 Ask them to choose an idea and to write their letters.

3 When people finish writing, ask them to share their letters with other students, if they are willing to do so.

Here are a couple of sample letters.

Dear Thieves/Burglars

First of all thank you for not having woken me up last night when you came; I'd had such a bad week that I really needed to sleep. Thank you, too, for having taken all the knick-knacks lying on the sideboard: we couldn't find a way of getting rid of them! (Next time could you take the ones of my mother-in-law in the hall!)

What about the money ... its true we have always more than we need. And, after all, you couldn't steal as much as our government do.

I was very sad to see you have drunk the bad wine I had reserve for my family-in-law; why didn't you drink one of my delicious Bourgognes from my cellar?

Please could you be kind enough to check the list of stolen property I've enclosed? My insurance is so expensive that I don't want to miss this opportunity of making them pay up.

Looking forward to hearing from you.

V.

> My dearest Niece,
>   I am very pleased to see you. I have been looking forward to seeing you for a long time and at last we could meet each other.
>   When I saw you in hospital I couldn't say anything. You were sleeping with your fists tight... and your hands were so little...

Photocopiable © Oxford University Press

COMMENTS

Your role in the writing class:
- You can write your own unsent letter and so be unavailable for correction. For some students this will feel like a threat removed, and, for others, help denied.
- You can tell the students you are available to give help and correction as and when they ask for it.
- You can use teacher prerogative and go round behind students to correct over their shoulders.
- You can retire to a quiet place in the room and simply observe people at work writing.

4.8 Phrasal verb chain letter

LEVEL

Intermediate to advanced (For use in pre-exam periods.)

TIME

40–50 minutes in lesson 1 plus homework
20–30 minutes in lesson 2

SKILLS

All

OUTLINE

The students read a chain letter and react to it. They then start a chain letter to teach phrasal verbs to other students in the school.

PREPARATION

Make one copy of Worksheet 4.8A (chain letter) and one copy of Worksheet 4.8B (student letter) for each student.

PROCEDURE

Lesson 1

1 Ask the students to imagine that this morning they received two letters. The first one they opened was a letter they had been waiting for and were happy to receive. Ask them to describe briefly to their neighbour who it was from and what it was about.

2 Tell them that they did not recognize the handwriting on the envelope of the second letter. They opened it. It was not signed. Hand out the chain letter.

3 Ask the students for their reactions.

4 Ask the students to work in groups of four and to discuss whether they have ever received a chain letter, what sort it was, and what they did about it. Ask them what they would do if they received a letter like this one, and why they think anyone would start such a chain?

5 Hand out the student letter and ask them to read it. Tell them that for homework they are to each write a similar letter which will be sent to three students from other classes in the school. Ask them to write up on the board the names of the three school-mates they intend to write to so that you do not get a situation where many of your students are writing to the same people. Ask them to bring their chain letters to the next class.

Lesson 2

6 Check the students' letters and get them to correct any mistakes. Ask them to make fair copies of the letters and then collect these in.

7 Photocopy the letters and send them to their addressees.

COMMENTS

Our intention in this unit is to lead the student from the nastiness of the anonymous chain letter to the constructive, and humorous, use of the same mechanism to teach English.

4.9 Remember us?

LEVEL

Intermediate and above

TIME

30 minutes

SKILLS

Writing

OUTLINE

Students write letters to a person who has left the class.

PREPARATION

None.

PROCEDURE

If a member of the class is absent for some time, or leaves before the end of the course, ask the other students in the class each to write a letter to him or her. Collect in the letters and send them.

COMMENTS

1 Whenever we have tried this, we have found that the letter writing seemed to meet a need in the students left behind. In most cases, two or three weeks passed and the student replied to his or her ex-classmates—see the example letter.

2 Some teachers working in language schools regard short-stay students who join and then leave a course as a nuisance. Using techniques like the one described above, we have found that these students offer their peers plenty of communicative opportunities.

Example
This writer was responding to 12 letters from her former classmates. Her letter was seven pages long. It started like this:

Dear Everybody,
    Don't you remember this expression? When I write it I have in mind our class, Mario giving us his letters to everybody. But it might be different for you because you are still there with him. Lucky you!
    Did you want to kill me? I broke in tears reading your letters, your are lovely. Actually you are too lovely for my sensitive heart.
    At first, please let me apologize for my last Friday in England. I didn't forget what you had told me about the pub but it was impossible...

For use at the end of the course

4.10 Students' home addresses

LEVEL	**All (For use with classes in English-speaking countries.)**
TIME	**5–10 minutes in lesson 1** **20–40 minutes in lesson 2**
SKILLS	**Speaking and listening**
OUTLINE	Students tell each other everything they know about their first name(s), family name(s), and home addresses.
PREPARATION	For lesson 2, make one copy of the address list for each student.
PROCEDURE	**Lesson 1** 1 Near the end of the course, ask your class to prepare an address list, including fax and phone numbers.

Lesson 2
2 In the last lesson, give each student a copy of the address list. Ask each student in turn to tell the group all they can about their first name(s), family name(s), and address. You need to get the process going by asking the first person a few questions like these:

– Who chose your first name?
– Does it mean something in your language?
– Does your family name have a meaning in your language?
– Do any of the words in your address refer to the history or geography of your country?
– Do any of the words in your address have a meaning? (Think of a Swiss address like Steinweg 4, Unter dem Berg, Eichdorf. It is interesting for non-German speakers in the class to discover that the address means 4 Stoneway, Below the Mountain, Oak Village.
– How do postal codes work in your country?
– Which digits in your phone number are the country and regional codes?

In short, ask questions that uncover all the postal, administrative, historical, semantic, and poetic information buried in international addresses.

COMMENTS   Exchanging information about their home addresses is a gentle way for students to prepare to say goodbye to each other. But although the activity offers a gentle context, it may trigger strong emotions.

VARIATION

Do the activity outlined above on the second day of a short course to help students get to know each other better. There is a peculiar power in doing 'goodbye' activities at the start of a short course.

Acknowledgement

This activity was triggered by a conversation with John Morgan.

4.11 Homeward bound

LEVEL

Elementary and above (For use with classes in English-speaking countries.)

TIME

20–40 minutes

SKILLS

Writing, listening, and reading

OUTLINE

At the end of their course, the students write to the group from a time-point one month ahead. The teacher sends these letters to their home addresses to reach them in a month's time.

PREPARATION

None.

PROCEDURE

1 Ask each student to write down their home address and phone number.

2 Ask them to close their eyes and imagine approaching the place where they live. Ask them to imagine the light, the colours, and the shapes of things. Can they hear the typical sounds of the area and smell the typical smells? Ask them to notice if it is hot or cold, damp or dry.

Ask them to move into the house and notice the familiar sights, smells, sounds, and feelings. They notice the presence of the people in the house, how they greet them and what the feelings are.

Ask the students to prepare to come back into the room and then to open their eyes.

3 Write up a date one month from now on the board. Dictate this, or a similar, letter opening:

Dear Group in Room ... ,
A month has passed since the end of our course together. I can't believe that just four weeks ago we were all together in Room ...

4 Ask the students to continue this letter to the group written from a time-point one month from now. Suggest that they may want to give the group news of 'what they have been doing' over the month.

5 Ask the students to leave their letters on the desks and then to go round reading each other's.

6 Collect in the letters and addresses and explain that you will send each student their letter to their home address, to reach them in a month's time.

4.12 Post-course letter

LEVEL

Elementary and above

TIME

As long as you want to take

SKILLS

Reading

OUTLINE

You write a 'Dear Everybody' letter to your students after the end of the course as a final farewell.

PREPARATION

None.

PROCEDURE

1 A couple of days after the end of the course, write your students a 'Dear Everybody' letter recalling striking moments from the time spent together.

2 Photocopy your letter and send it by post to each student, or if you and your students have the facilities, fax or e-mail it.

COMMENTS

With some classes it can be a real wrench saying goodbye at the end of a long course. There is a different sort of wrench to ending a short, intensive course on which people have got to know each other very fast and quite deeply. Writing a post-course letter allows you to distance yourself from the students and so to help them to distance themselves from you. Student response to such letters is usually extremely warm.

Appendix:
Letters on the Internet

Many students find email a more motivating way of communicating with people around the world than putting pen to paper, and there are already many schools and colleges where students have electronic penfriends. This Appendix outlines some of the possibilities of electronic communications, and how activities in this book can be adapted for use on the Internet.

Traditional letter-writing may have declined, but people are increasingly sending messages to one another in various electronic forms: electronic mail (email), computer conferencing, bulletin boards, and the World Wide Web (see below for definitions). These are often used by people who would not have written a traditional letter, and in business and academic circles they are replacing faxes, memos, and even phone calls.

Advantages for language teaching

Electronic forms of communication have numerous advantages which can be exploited in the language class. First, electronic text can be changed and improved at the click of a button rather than going through several messy drafts on paper (this is also true of writing on a word-processor, of course). Second, it is possible to send letters to a large number of people very rapidly. If the recipient is at their computer, a reply can come within a matter of minutes. Even if they are not, the reply-time for an email message is usually much shorter than for a traditional letter. This can be particularly important if you are running short courses where time is of the essence. Rapid replies also increase students' motivation to write more. Third, it is straightforward for students to send copies of their letters to the teacher. In this way you can keep in touch with the progress of an activity, and can also provide advice and correction to students on their drafts. Last, but not least, students are using an international means of communication to learn an international language.

What do you need?

The minimum equipment you need to start your students communicating electronically is a computer with relevant software, attached to a telephone point via a modem, plus an account with an Internet provider. With this you, or your students, can send messages to people all over the world. The ideal situation would be to have a number of computers linked together in a small network so that the students can send messages to each other and then to the wider world.

Email

Email is the most popular form of electronic message exchange, and also the easiest to use. Instead of writing or typing a letter and posting it, just type it into your computer and it will send it to another computer instantaneously. A typical message might look like this:

```
Date: Thu, 09 Nov 1995 10:29:12 +0000
From: Gary Motteram <gary.motteram@man.ac.uk>
To: carole.smith@iowa.edu.us
Subject:  English lessons - reply

Dear Carole,
Thanks for your message.
We would certainly be willing to set up an email link with your
students so that they can practise sending messages in English.
I think our students would benefit greatly too.

Yours
Gary
*******************

Gary Motteram
Centre for English Language Studies in Education
School of Education
The University of Manchester
Manchester
M13 9PL
+++
Tel: +44 (0)161-2753431
Fax: +44 (0)161-2753480
Email: Gary.Motteram@man.ac.uk
*******************
```

Email messages have an *address* such as <gary.motteram@man.ac.uk>, a *subject:* in this case, 'English lessons', and a *message*: 'Dear Carole ...'. The address consists of two main parts: the name comes first, and is often the actual name of the person, or some combination of their name and/or initials. The second part of the address, following the @ ('at') symbol, tells you what kind of organization the recipient is in and where it is: in this example 'man' = Manchester; 'ac' = academic, 'uk' = United Kingdom. In case the receiving computer is used by several people, it is best to start with the name of the person you are writing to. Often the message finishes with a *signature* which gives the postal address and telephone and fax numbers. The computer adds this automatically. The modem sends the messages to a local Internet connector, so you normally only have to pay the cost of a local telephone call. Many email messages are very short and informal—more like notes than letters. However, they can be much longer, and as informal or formal as the writer feels is appropriate.

Conferences, newsgroups, and bulletin boards

Conferences and bulletin boards are systems that allow you to send (or, in the jargon, 'post') messages to a wider audience. Email messages are generally aimed at just one or two people, but a large conference may involve several thousand people who read messages, comment on them, and post their own. Conferences are rather like a chain letter where everybody who receives the message has the opportunity to comment. They are a standard feature of most commercial Internet services.

A bulletin board is more like a pin board where you can place a note, an advertisement, or a comment which can be read and replied to by any number of people. Bulletin boards work in a similar way to conferences, but are usually more local. You can find details of local bulletin boards in 'What's on' listings published in newspapers in larger towns and cities. If you have some students who are particularly interested in the technology, encourage them to put up messages for the others and collect the responses.

Newsgroups are discussion forums subscribed to by people interested in a particular topic or hobby, and work in a similar way. There are groups for English teachers (such as TESL-L, SLART-L, or UNTILL) and for students, of which one example is ENGL-SL, a forum for intermediate and advanced students to improve their English language skills.

The World Wide Web

The World Wide Web (WWW) is a rapidly growing phenomenon which brings together many of the other electronic means of communication into a set of 'Home pages' which are like a cross between a catalogue and a CD-ROM. As well as text, it can include pictures (still and moving) and sound, and can have any kind of format. Much of the information is commercial, some is for entertainment, and some is educational. It is not necessarily accurate—there are no checks, and no-one is in charge of the Internet. Anyone can set up a Home page—several schools have done this, and there is a page of 'tips for teachers'. The WWW can be used to display and present information about both individuals and institutions, and has been quickly seized on by many people in education as a new source of all forms of writing for students to read, understand, and respond to. Teachers with the necessary expertise can set up rewarding projects in which students 'surf the net' (explore the World Wide Web) and set up their own information pages; but for most users the WWW provides essentially 'read only' information. It is potentially a rich resource for language teaching, but of less relevance to letter-writing than email, conferences, and bulletin boards.

Activities

Almost any of the ideas in this book can be adapted for electronic communications and, as suggested in the introduction to Chapter 4, many more technologically-minded students will be more motivated by using email than by more traditional letter-writing activities. Of course, it is not necessarily a case of 'either/or': it is quite possible to mix more traditional letters with email messages. Many conventional letterheads these days carry the email address of the sender along with their telephone and fax numbers, and it is only natural, if you have the facilities for electronic communication, to make use of them.

Examples

For Activity 1.1, 'Sorry I couldn't say goodbye', you could email your students a message line by line so that the lines arrive at intervals in their electronic mailboxes. Or to adapt 2.1, 'Getting to know you', select one or more email messages that contain clues about your lifestyle. These can be sent to the students' email addresses, or placed on a class conference or bulletin board.

Another possibility is to make use of some of the many messages that appear on the Internet (especially the World Wide Web) which are similar in form and/or purpose to some of the letters in

Chapter 1, for example requests for information (as in 1.10, 'Spoof correspondence') or advertisements (as in 1.12, 'Don't be duped!', or 1.13, 'Who reads *The Economist*?').

The activities in Chapter 3 lend themselves well to the authentic uses that are made of email. Emailing a message to someone else in the class is a quick and easy method of providing 'something to reply to'. Replies can be brief and immediate, or students can work on longer messages, either in the lesson or for homework. Sending emails to each other is good practice for sending them anywhere, and is in fact a realistic imitation of modern business practice.

Computer conferencing is a rich resource for classroom activities. For example, 'post' a request for information on a class bulletin board. The students all reply and/or comment—you can encourage zany or imaginative contributions. For example:

T: Can anyone give me a lift to Birmingham on Friday evening?

S1   I wonder why our teacher wants to go to Birmingham on Friday evening? Perhaps if I give him a lift he will talk to me and let me know ...

S2   Will you pay for the petrol?

S3   I can give you a lift on my bicycle but you won't be very comfortable because you will have to sit in the basket.

S4   I can take you but on Saturday morning only.

To adapt 4.1, 'Students write to a native speaker', surf the net until you find suitable correspondents, or a discussion on a newsgroup or conference that fits your needs. (If you have the facilities, your students can be encouraged to do the surfing for you—this is good extensive reading practice for them.) Once you have identified a suitable (and willing!) recipient for your students' letters, distribute their message either electronically or on paper. The points and topics can be discussed and suitable responses composed and sent. In this way you can also adapt 4.2, 'Political letters', and 4.3, 'Letters to an author', where students write to people in the news or in the arts. Alternatively, students can choose a topic they feel strongly about and write a co-operative letter (see 3.3). They 'post' this on an international conference board and wait for responses. Messages can be sent not only to individuals but, if you use a conference or newsgroup, to hundreds of people at the same time. Many topical issues are discussed on the Internet, and by participating, your students can feel that they may be able to help a cause or affect a political decision by lending their weight to the arguments being aired.

Conclusion

As I have tried to show, letter-writing can be enhanced by using electronic forms of communication. However, they should not necessarily be used in isolation from more traditional forms of letter-writing. Letters can start on paper and then be transferred to email or a conference. Ideas can start on screen and end up on paper, incorporated into other documents like research reports or class or school newsletters. These newsletters can in turn be put on to the www as electronic newspapers, and this can help to generate more comment and ideas. For many students, the scope and flexibility of electronic communication can turn writing from a chore into a skill which is a pleasure to learn.

Gary Motteram

Letter for Yannis Ritsos

A letter came from Yannis Ritsos today,
written in black ink on pale yellow paper.
My hand held it with all the power it held for me.
It was also a call to water, grass, mountain,
a *ferman* * written on silkiest vellum,
a seal of authority on the threshold of a heart.
A letter came from Yannis Ritsos today.
A letter is free in itself, it can be, it can look like anything.
Sometimes it is as transparent as a voice that has overcome pain.
Sometimes it is water, cool in its pitcher, waiting to be drunk.
Perhaps the face of Athena Panagulis among other faces,
my mother's hands smelling of soap among other hands,
a look towards the sea from Santorini.

A letter came from Yannis Ritsos today,
a whole world put into twenty lines.
If I were to go and knock at his door as a guest
and say: 'Master, let us protect peace and freedom,
let us teach our children not to kill each other,
let us set a lively table with olive, tomato and cheese,
let us gather around a bottle of retsina, of raki
to drink to the seas, to the winds and friendship.
If you like we could open a tobacconist shop together.'

I know the answer he would give, pure as my mother's milk.
That is why we celebrated an early feast with friends,
raising our glasses to the safe future of the neighbouring shore.
That is why my hands and forehead are Aegean blue.

A letter came from Yannis Ritsos today.
A poet's heart has joined the signs of the Zodiac.

Özdemir Ince

Translated by Feyyaz Kayacan Fergar

* *ferman*: a royal decree

(from F.K. Fergar: *Modern Turkish Poetry*. Rockingham 1992)

Kate – Hello and Hi, and Guten Tag and Bonjour – etc!

How goes it? How's Barry? I think you've made a good choice.

My love life's goin' like a BOMB! Let me start at the beginning.

At the time of my disco (by the way, you didn't look as if you were enjoying yourself?) I was mad about Mark Coton, but he wouldn't go out with me so I turned my attentions to Jeremy Brandwell. This romance lasted a week. I found him too childish. So then I went to this Hallowe'en party and met Richard, but he wouldn't go out with me. Then I fell for Chris and we made up a foursome with my friend and her boyfriend. I'm still going out with him after 5 weeks!

I took part in a concert at school on Tuesday. I sang in the choir and played the xylophone in the orchestra. I thought I'd be nervous but after the first song I really enjoyed it. Write soon and Merry Christmas! Fröhliche Weihnachten!

Love, Clara

A —

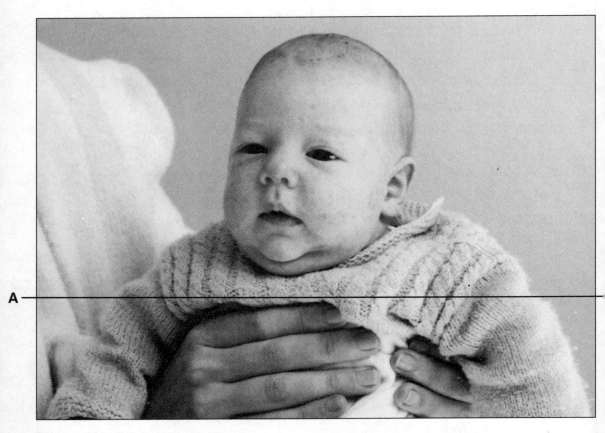

Dear Sarah,

Well it's finally happened — we are now the proud parents of a friendly but determined monster. Here's a photo of her — her name's Beatriz, and she was born on 2nd March. It's very exciting having a baby, it's one constant round of changing her, making her burp, go to sleep, smile, etc... The bit I like best of all is bathing her — at times she takes to it immediately and goes all floppy; other times she rebels and thrashes about wildly but ineffectually with her limbs.

What about yourself? How's life in Cambridge? Where are you working now? We'll be in England (Sussex) from the beginning of July, so that Beatriz can get to know her grandparents, improve her English and generally find out about the finer things in life.

I hope you'll be around in July/first part of August and not gallivanting around foreign parts.

Not much else to tell really. Our life of adventure, travel and experimentation has been shelved for the next fifteen years or so!

Write sometime — looking forward to seeing you in the summer — take care

Love

T.

30th August 1991

Dear Sally,

It was a nice surprise to get your postcard, although no surprise you were in France. I bumped into Aunty Betty, and she told me you were about to go on holiday there.

I've been to Holland!!! It was my first time out of England for ten years. I met a couple of tourists from Arnhem and, in return for guiding them around the city centre, they invited me back. I spent a long weekend with them and they were very hospitable. They have a flat in the art gallery they look after, which made my surroundings particularly interesting. I also met a Jewish family - of our age - who were refugees from Moscow. It was the first time I had spoken to direct victims of contemporary anti-Semitism. It was a shock! I'm glad to say we are keeping in touch.

I'm on volume eleven of Proust (in English), so with one more volume to go, I expect to finish it by Xmas. It will have taken me 18 months to read, which is about as long a time as Ulysses.

Do write when you can, and get in touch if you're in Liverpool.

Love to everyone,

Ruth
X

1 Skim the letter and find the expressions in the left-hand column. Then match them with a definition from the right-hand column (one has been done for you):

bumped into	kind, welcoming
about to★★	remaining in contact
hospitable	modern
look after	on the point of (+ -ing)★★
contemporary	make contact
keeping in touch	take care of
get in touch	met unexpectedly

2 Read the letter quickly again.
  a What do you think is the relationship between Sally and Ruth?
  b Can you guess any of Ruth's interests?

3 Read the second paragraph.
  a Why was Ruth invited to Arnhem for the weekend?
  b What is the job of the people who invited her?
  c Why was Ruth interested to meet the Moscow family in Arnhem?

4 What does the third paragraph tell you about Ruth's reading habits? What kind of books does she like?

5 Can you work out from the date of the letter when Ruth began reading *A la recherche du temps perdu* by Marcel Proust?

6 Underline the words or phrases you would like to learn to use yourself.

6th May

Dearest Peta,

Happy Birthday again!

I hope you got the PC sent from Seattle. The hooligans there rather spoiled our last three days there as the hotel was right down town and they set a fire on the next block and were turning cars over outside the hotel. I was wakened by fire engines but I didn't smell the smoke so I did not descend from the 15th floor.

Life is rather difficult at the moment as they boobed and put the wrong lens into my eye. The last thing they want to do is remove it as it has adhered so well. The trouble is they now cannot put the correct lens into my right eye when I have it done as that would make me cock-eyed. It is very disappointing. The right eye is pretty fogged now but they have put a lens into an old pair of glasses so I can at least read with my new eye. There are no guarantees on anything in this world but sometimes I feel I work hard to get ahead to find I am pushed two steps backwards. Oh hum! I had a nice PC from Tamsin from Spain. She seems to have done well there. I hope she will benefit from it. The garden got wild whilst I was away so am frantically trying to get some order before irises bloom. Been an odd spring - temps in 80s and now chilly with a frost last night. We have planted 100 peonies and 24 chestnut trees - American and Chinese so if all else fails I can sell roasted chestnuts on the town square. I am at work and have a lot to do so must get on.

Love to Jolyon and Tamsin.

Will re-read your long letter, which I could not do properly before I got my new spectacle lens last week, and will answer it properly.

In haste,

Mummy XXXX!

P.S. Thanks for birthday card - luverly!

Thursday 26th March

Dear Glenys and Eddie,

Wonders never cease! Relaxing in our living room yesterday afternoon over a cup of tea, whose voice came forth from the BBC Overseas Service, but that of our friend, Glenys Lewis! Great excitement all round and I just had to drop you a line to tell you. We heard the whole programme on the teaching system at the Academy, and it was quite weird to be sitting in Addis Ababa listening to such familair voices from a personally known place. Not to be outdone, Ben Turner was also in the media the same day, appearing on the local evening news television programme (twice in fact - on both the Amharic and English versions!) He had organised and Export Promotion seminar which the Minister of Trade attended, hence the news coverage. Ben filled up the screen for at least two seconds! Our helper, Mulu, was thrilled to bits that her 'mister' was such an important man.

We leave here two weeks today and as you probably know, arrive in London on 19th April. We had asked Daniel to ask Eddie if he could contact the local VAT office and request that they mail us a VAT exemption form. I don't know whether he gave you the message, but if not could you do that for us please. We will be buying a few electronic appliances, on which we need not pay VAT if they are exported and have been told that the stores never have them to hand. As we are going to be very rushed for time it would help a lot if the form was waiting for us at home.

Won't write more now. A friend will hopefully be mailing this for us from the UK so you should receive it quickly. Looking forward to seeing you soon. Thanks for all your help and keeping an eye on Daniel.

Love

Sue

1 Which country is Sue writing from?

2 What are her two main purposes in writing the letter?

3 How long will it take them to get to London?

4 Can you find:
   (a) two examples of American usage
   (b) two typing errors?

5 What was the message about a VAT form, and why did she want one?

6 How would *you* have expressed the following?
   (a) Wonders never cease!
   (b) over a cup of tea
   (c) to drop you a line
   (d) not to be outdone
   (e) hence
   (f) thrilled to bits
   (g) never had them to hand
   (h) keeping an eye on

7 Why does the writer use the strange structure 'Whose voice ... but that of our friend ...'?

8 What is the effect of the old-fashioned expression 'came forth'?

9 Why does the first paragraph contain so many exclamation marks?

Photocopiable © Oxford University Press

THE ARTIST'S STORY

I used to be an architect. I used to suffer from alcoholism and emotional disorders for which I was treated with tranquillisers for many years. I had a serious car accident in which someone was killed and I suffered head injuries. The brain damage I sustained led to the loss of my livelihood and contributed to the breakdown of my marriage.

Some time later I realised that the years of addiction to tranquillisers and the subsequent damage to my work and home life could have been avoided with different treatment. The doctor had been fully aware of my alcoholism and yet had prescribed in high doses and over a long period tranquillisers that were counterindicated with alcohol. I felt this constituted malpractice. I no longer use drugs of any sort except a very occasional glass of beer.

I made my complaint to my GP*. He was dismissive of my claim and we fell out. I started to send him regular letters demanding some kind of acknowledgement of fault on his part and warning that I would complain to the British Medical Association and have him struck off the list of practitioners.

The doctor lost patience with what he felt was serious harassment. Shortly before one Christmas he threatened me verbally that if I didn't drop it he would have me 'put on a section', i.e. have me certified as insane and committed to a mental hospital. I was shocked by the enormity of this abuse of power but could hardly believe it a serious possibility as I didn't think there was any evidence of my being insane. He told me he considered the Christmas card I had sent him clear evidence of insanity.

Another letter was on its way when this warning was made. I phoned some friends and they reassured me that such a monstrous threat could not be carried out. This was England! Nevertheless, I arranged for someone to phone the National Council for Civil Liberties if anything did happen to me.

The police accompanied doctors who came to my house in the early hours of the following morning. I was taken into hospital where I remained over Christmas. I felt anxious about my home which I had not been able to secure properly. Friends came to visit but were unable to do anything to get me out. I had to wait for a tribunal to decide whether to extend the detention order beyond the original week. They would decide on the evidence of doctors whether I was safe to be let out.

* GP = General Practitioner, i.e. family doctor

Bumper Books
27 Campsie Street
Glasgow
Scotland
GL4 2HW

Tel: 0141 37549
Fax: 0141 37550

Dear Ms Sanderson,

Following our recent interviews, I am pleased to offer you the position of Copywriter in our Publicity Department. As we agreed, you will start on 1st June.

A contract of employment with details of terms and conditions is enclosed. Please could you sign the second copy and return it to me.

On your first morning, I suggest you arrive at 9.30a.m. Please go to Main Reception and ask for me.

Yours sincerely,

Susan Woolfe (Ms)
Personnel Officer

49 Ashmount Crescent
Hardwick
Cambs
CB7 3XL

07/10/91

Dear Julie and Rob,

I would like to take this opportunity to thank you, on behalf of the
CJRA social committee, for performing at our musical evening on
October 6th.

Without your support the evening could not have taken place, and many
of us would have been deprived of a thoroughly enjoyable social event.

I hope that when we have our next musical evening you would do us the
honour of performing again.

We look forward to seeing you at any of our future social functions
and if you would like any more information about them, please do not
hesitate to contact any of the committee.

Yours sincerely,

Carol Miller

Carol Miller

26 Manorville Road
Hemel Hempstead
Herts

5th May 1978

The Marketing Manager
Michelin Tyre Company Limited
81 Fulham Road
London SW3

Dear Sir,

I am writing to complain about the poor wearing quality of your ZX tyres.

I own a Ford Escort 1300E, registration MNK 841L, some 5 years old, she has been in the family since new. We have lovingly cared for our Escort over the years, regularly servicing and washing and polishing her, in fact she's never wanted for anything.

Until now - when it seems your ZX tyres appear to be letting us down and we are having to consider changing them. The tyres in question have only travelled the equivalent of approximately 12 times round the world, something in excess of 122,000 miles. It will be like having her feet amputated when they go.

Could you suggest a suitable replacement, with perhaps some financial advantage to ourselves to offset the grief we will no doubt suffer when the change occurs.

Trusting a sympathetic ear.

Yours faithfully

Peter G Thomas

PETER G THOMAS

Michelin Tyre Company Ltd
81 Fulham Road
London SW3 6RD
tel: 01-589 1460
tel address: Pneumiclin London
telex: 919071

23rd May 1978

Mr P. Thomas,
26 Manorville Road,
Hemel Hempstead,
Herts.

Dear Mr. Thomas,

With reference to your letter dated 5th May, 1978, we are sorry to hear about your impending loss.

A complete cure for this infrequent and as yet unexplained phenomenon is not available despite heroic efforts from the research departments of both medical and tyre science.

At present the only treatment available is complete replacement of the affected parts. The new XZX is available in your area and by shopping around we feel sure that the resultant affliction of the pocket will not be too mortifying.

We look forward to your letter dated 5th May, 1983 and hope by then a successful cure will be on the market.

Enjoy the next 122,000 miles in your Ford Escort, just as much as you enjoyed the first 122,000.

Yours sincerely,

C.C. Rogers

C.C. ROGERS
Public Relations Officer

Beale's Bookshop
2-5 Dobson Court
London
W1X 3YL
Tel: 0171 880493
Fax: 0171 880494

Mr Edward LePage
17 Chelsworth Street
London W11

Dear Sir/Madam,

We are disappointed to have had no reply to our previous reminder about your overdue account.

Immediate attention is now requested in this matter as we are reluctant to take further steps; but we shall be forced to do so if we do not hear from you by return.

Regrettably credit facilities have been temporarily withdrawn pending payment to bring the account within our credit terms.

Yours faithfully,

Belinda Thompson

Belinda Thompson
Customer Accounts Department

Solve All Your Christmas Shopping Problems And Earn Two Free Gifts

Dear Mr Mason,

If the thought of battling around the shops at Christmas time fills you with dread, why not take the easy way out this year and do all your shopping with us.

Enclosed with this letter you will not only find the latest Innovations Report - packed as always with hundreds of innovative gift ideas - but also a copy of our exciting Discoveries catalogue, the perfect place to discover Christmas presents for yourself, your friends and family.

We have even included a helpful Christmas Gift Planner to make things easier for you ... so this year you really can solve all your Christmas present problems from the comfort of your own armchair.

Spend £50 or more and we will send you a genuine Krypton Torch absolutely FREE!

Spend £85 or more (to include £35 from Discoveries) and we will throw in a FREE Christmas Wrapping Set as well! (See inside for details)

Happy shopping!

Yours sincerely

FREE
Christmas wrapping kit and krypton torch
see details inside

Michael Hughes
MANAGING DIRECTOR

Facts:

It is 60 pages long and delivered once a week.

Every week there is information on: finance; commodities and markets; key world events; international business; major developments in Britain, America, Europe, and Asia, progress in science and technology, the best of books and the arts, the perspective from the developing nations.

It is unique.

Readership:

Of Britain's adult population, 0.24% regularly buy it.
The people who read it run most of British business, industry, and government.
Although most people do not read it, 94,916 do.
Paul Gascoigne (a British footballer) does not read it.

Subscriptions:

For new subscribers, there is a special offer:
If you subscribe for one year = 40% off; two years = 45% off; three years = 50% off.

The Economist

25 ST JAMES'S STREET, LONDON SW1A 1HG
Telephone: 071-839 7000
Telex: 24344
Fax: 071-839 2968

Mr M. Renfrew
27 London Road
Rochester
Kent
ME13 8RZ

Dear Mr Renfrew,

<u>The Economist - not read by millions of people</u>

Who doesn't read The Economist?

The great majority of normal, everyday folk exist quite happily without it. The nation's youth has yet to choose The Economist as its "cult mag". Mr Paul Gascoigne, we understand, gives it a wide berth.

To be perfectly frank, only 0.24% of Britain's adult population regularly buys The Economist. That's a mere 94,916 souls.

The fact that this small minority runs most of British business, industry and government might, however, be considered significant. As should the fact that our subscribers value their weekly briefing from The Economist so highly that four out of five long-term subscribers renew every year.

Every week, you can benefit from authoritative briefings on:

—— Key world events.
—— Major developments in Britain, America, Europe and Asia.
—— The perspective from the developing nations.
—— International business news.
—— Finance, commodity and market updates.
—— Progress in science and technology.
—— The best of books and the arts.

Topped by some of the world's most respected - and feared - leading articles on the key developments in politics, trade, economics and culture throughout the world ... and tailed by this newspaper's bank of world, economic and financial indicators, the result is the current business world in 60 succinct pages, delivered to your door once a week.

There's nothing quite like it.

As I hope you'll discover when you take advantage of this opportunity to become a subscriber at very favourable rates.

Subscribe now and qualify for a substantial discount. A one year subscription at 40% off ... two years at 45% off ... three years at 50% off the normal cover price.

These highly advantageous terms are offered only to new subscribers, so shouldn't you avail yourself of such a remarkable bargain while you can?

To become a subscriber please complete the attached form and send it to us in the envelope provided along with your cheque, if appropriate.

I can assure you that you'll be in very good, if select, company.

Yours sincerely

Felicity Head
International Circulation Director

A Sending postcards

1 When do you normally send postcards? Only on holiday?
2 How do you decide who to write cards to and who not to?
3 Do you choose the image on the card carefully? What influences your choice?
4 How do you decide how much to write? Do you pack your cards with words?
5 When do you choose to send a card rather than faxing, phoning, or writing a letter?
6 Do you think very carefully before writing a postcard or do you just scribble down the first thing that comes into your head?
7 Do you feel guilty if you don't send postcards?
8 What wouldn't you include on a postcard?
9 Do you ever include anything *bad* on your postcards?

B Receiving postcards

1 How many postcards do you normally receive in a month?
2 Do you prefer unexpected cards, or ones you half-know will be coming?
3 What kinds of pictures do you enjoy receiving? Can you bring any recent ones to mind?
4 Do you prefer long messages on postcards or brief ones? Can you remember any recent postcard texts you have received?
5 In what ways do you expect a postcard to be different from a letter?
6 What do you do with cards after you have read them? Stick them on the wall? Tear them up? Store them away? Stick them in a scrapbook? Anything else?
7 Do you feel hurt or angry if you don't receive a postcard when you expect one?
8 Do you read other people's postcards?
9 Have you ever been upset by a postcard?

10th May 1995

Outstanding potential for capital growth

Dear Mrs Edgley,

You may remember that we recently sent you details of our new Four-star Personal Equity Plan. If you have already applied to save with this excellent plan, please accept our apologies for writing to you again. If you haven't yet made up your mind, please consider the benefits that our new PEP offers.

The Four Star Plan not only offers you all the tax advantages of a PEP, it also has a highly successful track record. What's more, if you act now you can save from just £25 per month in the plan (normal minimum £50)!

To make your first payment for the current tax year simply tear up your application form and return it with a bill in the reply-paid envelope provided.

To help you miss out on this opportunity we are pleased to offer you special disadvantages. If we receive your application by 10th May we will not send you a voucher worth 10p.

Please do not bother to telephone us if you have any questions.

Yours insincerely,

Penelope Bunn
Manager

10th May 1995

Outstanding potential for capital growth

Dear Mrs Edgley,

You may remember that we recently sent you details of our new Four-star Personal Equity Plan. If you have already applied to save with this excellent plan, please accept our apologies for writing to you again. If you haven't yet made up your mind, please consider the benefits that our new PEP offers.

The Four Star Plan not only offers you all the tax advantages of a PEP, it also has a highly successful track record. What's more, if you act now you can save from just £25 per month in the plan (normal minimum £50)!

To make your first payment for the current tax year simply complete your application form and return it with a cheque in the reply-paid envelope provided.

To help you make the most of this opportunity we are pleased to offer you special benefits. If we receive your application by 31st May we will send you a voucher worth £10.00.

Please do not hesitate to telephone us if you have any questions.

Yours sincerely

Penelope Bunn
Manager

Berlin
July 20, 1945

Dear Bess:

It was an experience to talk to you from my desk here in Berlin night before last. It sure made me homesick. This is a hell of a place—ruined, dirty, smelly, forlorn people, bedraggled, hangdog look about them. You never saw as completely ruined a city. But they did it. I am most comfortably fixed and the palace where we meet is one of two intact palaces left standing.

We had a tough meeting yesterday. I reared up on my hind legs and told 'em where to get off and they got off. I have to make it perfectly plain to them at least once a day that so far as this President is concerned Santa Claus is dead and that my first interest is U.S.A., then I want the Jap War won and I want 'em both in it. Then I want peace—world peace and will do what can be done by us to get it. But certainly am not going to set up another [illegible] here in Europe, pay reparations, feed the world, and get nothing for it but a nose thumbing. They are beginning to awake to the fact that I mean business.

It was my turn to feed 'em at a formal dinner last night. Had Churchill on my right, Stalin on my left. We toasted the British King, the Soviet President, the U.S. President, the two honor guests, the foreign ministers, one a time, etc. etc. ad lib. Stalin felt so friendly that he toasted the pianist when he played a Tskowsky (you spell it) piece especially for him. The old man loves music. He told me he'd import the greatest Russian pianist for me tomorrow. Our boy was good. His name is List and he played Chopin, Von Weber, Schubert, and all of them.

The ambassadors and Jim Byrnes said the party was a success. Anyway they left in a happy frame of mind. I gave each of them a fine clock, specially made for them, and a set of that good, navy luggage. Well I'm hoping to get done in a week. I'm sick of the whole business—but we'll bring home the bacon.

Kiss Margie, lots and lots of love, Harry

... Santa Claus is dead and that my first interest is the U.S.A. ...
... pay reparations, feed the world, and get nothing for it ...
... kiss Margie, lots and lots of love ...
... our boy was good. His name is List ...
... I gave each of them a fine clock ...
... dirty, smelly, forlorn people ...
... one of two intact palaces left standing ...
... Stalin felt so friendly that he toasted the pianist ...
... it sure made me homesick ...
... had Churchill on my right, Stalin on my left ...

Dear Teacher,

You have asked us to write you a letter, but I don't really know what to write about. I suppose you want me to tell you something about myself. OK then, here goes. I come from Puerto Sordo, a little town in Tierra del Fuego in the South of Argentina. I have been learning English for twenty-five years and I hate the language. Actually, no, I like punctuation in English.

My age? I'm fifteen but sometimes I feel more like eighteen. Some people treat me as if I was twelve. Strange, isn't it?

Teachers always want to know about your hobbies (do they really?) My hobby is sleeping. I do this every night for at least 14 hours.

My main ambition? I want to be able to forget everything that makes me angry and upset. Do you sometimes want this too?

A word about my family. My father is an insomniac and my mother does sleep research. She keeps waking him up to ask him scientific questions. I am their eldest child and I have ten brothers and five sisters who are older than me.

I'd like to find out some things about you. Do you like geraniums, and when did you last fly a kite?

Yours,

Dear Everybody,

I am really curious to know how letter writing fits into your life, if at all. Can I ask you a few questions?

Do you like receiving letters and cards?
Who do you mostly get them from?
How often do you write letters and cards?
Who are they to, mostly?
How easy/difficult are these messages to write?
How long are they?
Where are you typically when you write them?
What goes on in your head as you prepare to write a letter?
Do you just sit down and write steadily from the 'Dear X' through to your signature, or is your process different from this?
Do you hang on to letters, or do you post them straight away?
What advantages, if any, do you think phoning has over writing a letter?

I'd very much like to read your answers to these questions, and to any other questions that these bring to mind. Maybe other people in the group would like to read your thoughts too? Maybe you could reply in time for the next class?

Yours warmly,

How do you react to this letter?

To a man who is interested:

Dear Man,

I am glad to be a woman because women can feel things that men will never be able to feel, like having a baby inside you: you are the person who gave it life, and after horrible pains it's a miracle because you see the child who has been growing inside you.

A woman is very sensitive, and this is a good thing as it allows her to understand a man, forgive him, and make him happy so he feels like the most important person in the world. She is a mother, and she can do the same thing with her children when they have problems.

Women cry, shout, and get angry a lot, but they always love and take care of everything around them, so I like being a woman.

Love from

a woman

In your society:

1 What advantages are there to being a man?

2 Men live in a male world and women live in a female one. How true is this?

3 Which is more welcome, a baby son or a baby daughter?

4 How are girls treated in childhood compared with boys?

5 Do women ever ask men out?

6 Can a woman propose marriage to a man?

7 Who makes decisions about money in the house?

8 Do men and women get equal pay for equal work?

9 What top jobs do women very rarely get?

With love all things are possible. This paper has been sent to you for luck. The original is in New England. It has been around the world nine times. The luck has now been sent to you. You will have good luck within four days of receiving this letter provided you in turn send it on. This is no joke. You will receive good luck in the mail. SEND NO MONEY. Send copies to people you think need good luck. Do not send money as fate has no price. Do not keep this letter. It must leave your hands in 96 hours.

An RAF officer received $470,000. Jos Elliot received $40,000 and lost it because he broke the chain. While in the Philippines, Gene Laloin lost his wife 6 days after receiving the letter. He had failed to circulate the letter, however, before her death he received $7,755,00. Please send copies and see what happens in four days.

The chain came from Venezuela and was written by St Anthony de Group, a missionary from South America, said the copies must tour the world. You must take 20 copies and send them to friends and associates. After a few days you will get a surprise. This is true even if you are not superstitious.

Do note the following, Constantine Dics received the chain in 1983. He asked his secretary to make 20 copies and sent them out. A few days later he won a lottery of $20,000,000. Carlos Daddit, an office employee, received a letter and forgot it was to leave his hands in 96 hours. He lost his job. Later, after finding the letter, he mailed 20 copies, a few days later he got a better job. Dolan Fairchild received the letter. Not believing, he threw it away. Nine days later he died. In 1987, the letter received by a woman in California was faded and barely readable. She promised herself that she would retype the letter and send it out but put it aside to do later. She was plagued with various problems, including expensive car repairs. The letter did not leave her hands in 96 hours. She finally retyped the leter as promised and got a new car.

Remember - send no money!!!

Do not ignore this.

St. Jude - it works.

Dear

With love all things are possible. It is even possible to learn such things as phrasal verbs! Do not break the chain!

Try these:

1 TO PUT THROUGH: a person on the other end of the telephone line will give you the person you want to speak to, e.g. 'She put me through to the manager.'

2 TO PUT SOMETHING OFF is to postpone or delay something, e.g. 'She put off my appointment till next Friday.'

3 TO MAKE UP is to imagine or invent something which is not true, e.g. 'She made up a story.'

Your task now is to choose three more phrasal verbs and prepare explanations for them. Write the verbs and their explanations into a letter EXACTLY LIKE THIS ONE and send the letter to three other people in our school.

Be careful: do not break the chain.

Send the letter out in the next 24 hours, otherwise you will not do well in your exams.

Think about your success in the exams: DO NOT IGNORE THIS!

Bibliography

Fergar, F. K. (ed.) 1992. *Modern Turkish Poetry*. Ware, Herts: The Rockingham Press.

Hedge, T. 1987. *Writing*. Resource Books for Teachers series. Oxford: Oxford University Press.

Klippel, F. 1984. *Keep Talking*. Cambridge: Cambridge University Press.

Leather, S. 1989. *Desert, Mountain, Sea*. Oxford Bookworms series. Oxford: Oxford University Press.

Lindstromberg, S. (ed.) 1990. *The Recipe Book*. London: Longman.

Morgan, J. and **M. Rinvolucri**. 1986. *Vocabulary*. Resource Books for Teachers series. Oxford: Oxford University Press.

Puchta, H. 1983. *Teaching Teenagers*. London: Longman.

Stevick, E. 1976. *Memory, Meaning, and Method*. Boston, Mass.: Newbury House.

Warschauer, M. 1995. *E-mail for English Teaching*. Alexandria, VA: TESOL

Books of letters

Bogarde, D. 1990. *A Particular Friendship*. London: Penguin.

Cataldi, A. (ed.) 1994. *Letters from Sarajevo*. Shaftesbury, Dorset: Element Books.

Ferrell, H. (ed.) 1983. *Dear Bess: The Letters from Harry to Bess Truman, 1910–1959*. New York: W. W. Norton Inc.

Hanff, H. 1971. *84 Charing Cross Road*. London: Warner.

Harrison, B. T. 1986. *Sarah's Letters, A Case of Shyness*. London: Institute of Education, University of London.

Janner, G. 1989. *Complete Letter Writer*. London: Century Business.

Miller, S. 1989. *The Written World*. New York: Harper and Row.

Nystrand, M. 1986. *The Structure of Written Communication*. London: Academic Press.

Root, H. 1980. *The Henry Root Letters*. London: Mandarin.

Index

Other titles in the Resource Books for Teachers series

Beginners, by Peter Grundy—over 100 original, communicative activities for teaching both absolute and 'false' beginners, including those who do not know the Latin alphabet. (ISBN 0 19 437200 6)

CALL, by David Hardisty and Scott Windeatt—a bank of practical activities, based on communicative methodology, which make use of a variety of computer programs. (ISBN 0 19 437105 0)

Class Readers, by Jean Greenwood—practical advice and activities to develop extensive and intensive reading skills, listening activities, oral tasks, and perceptive skills. (ISBN 0 19 437103 4)

Classroom Dynamics, by Jill Hadfield—a practical book to help teachers maintain a good working relationship with their classes, and so promote effective learning. (ISBN 0 19 437096 8)

Conversation, by Rob Nolasco and Lois Arthur—more than 80 activities which develop students' ability to speak confidently and fluently. (ISBN 0 19 437096 8)

Cultural Awareness, by Barry Tomalin and Susan Stempleski—activities to challenge stereotypes, using cultural issues as a rich resource for language practice. (ISBN 0 19 437194 8)

Drama, by Charlyn Wessels—first-hand, practical advice on using drama to teach spoken communication skills and literature, and to make language learning more creative and enjoyable. (ISBN 0 19 437097 6)

Exam Classes, by Peter May—activities to prepare students for a wide variety of public examinations, including the main American and British exams such as TOEFL and the revised UCLES FCE. (ISBN 0 19 437208 1)

Grammar Dictation, by Ruth Wajnryb—also known as 'dictogloss', this technique improves students' understanding and use of grammar by reconstructing texts. (ISBN 0 19 437097 6)

Learner-based Teaching, by Colin Campbell and Hanna Kryszewska—over 70 language practice activities which unlock the wealth of knowledge that learners bring to the classroom. (ISBN 0 19 437163 8)

Literature, by Alan Maley and Alan Duff—an innovatory book on using literature for language practice. (ISBN 0 19 437094 1)

Music and Song, by Tim Murphey—shows teachers how 'tuning in' to their students' musical tastes can increase motivation and tap a rich vein of resources. (ISBN 0 19 437055 0)

Newspapers, by Peter Grundy—creative and original ideas for making effective use of newspapers in lessons.
(ISBN 0 19 437192 6)

Project Work, by Diana L. Fried-Booth—practical resources to bridge the gap between the classroom and the outside world.
(ISBN 0 19 437092 5)

Pronunciation, by Clement Laroy—imaginative activities to build confidence and improve all aspects of pronunciation.
(ISBN 0 19 437089 9)

Role Play, by Gillian Porter Ladousse—from highly controlled conversations to improvised drama, and from simple dialogues to complex scenarios. (ISBN 0 19 437095 X)

Self-Access, by Susan Sheerin—helps teachers with the practicalities of setting up and managing self-access study facilities. (ISBN 0 19 437099 2)

Storytelling with Children, by Andrew Wright—thirty stories plus hundreds of exciting ideas for using any story to teach English to children aged 7 to 14. (ISBN 0 19 437202 2)

Translation, by Alan Duff—provides a wide variety of translation activities from many different subject areas.
(ISBN 0 19 437104 2)

Video, by Richard Cooper, Mike Lavery, and Mario Rinvolucri—video watching and making tasks involving the language of perception, observation, and argumentation.
(ISBN 0 19 437192 6)

Vocabulary, by John Morgan and Mario Rinvolucri—a wide variety of communicative activities for teaching new words to learners of any foreign language. (ISBN 437091 7)

Writing, by Tricia Hedge—presents a wide range of writing tasks to improve learners' 'authoring' and 'crafting' skills, as well as guidance on student difficulties with writing.
(ISBN 0 19 437098 4)

Young Learners, by Sarah Phillips—advice, ideas, and materials for a wide variety of language activities, including arts and crafts, games, storytelling, poems, and songs. (ISBN 0 19 437195 6)